BACKSTAGE GUIDE™
— TO —
REAL ESTATE

BACKSTAGE GUIDE™

— TO —

REAL ESTATE

Produce Passive Income,
Write Your Own Story,
and Direct Your Dollars
Toward Positive Change

MATT PICHENY

SLOAN ROSE
——— PUBLISHING ———

contact@sloanrosepublishing.com

ISBN: 978-1-7375384-0-0 (paperback)
ISBN: 978-1-7375384-2-4 (hardcover)
ISBN: 978-1-7375384-1-7 (ebook)
ISBN: 978-1-7375384-3-1 (audiobook)

Ordering Information:
Special discounts are available on quantity purchases by corporations, associations, and others. For details, please email contact@sloanrosepublishing.com

DEDICATION

"

To my mother, Sandra Picheny, and the memory of my father, Robert Picheny,
whose legacy values and entrepreneurial spirit I am proud to carry forward.

To my incredible wife, Erica, and our amazing daughters, Julia and Abby.
You inspire me to be better every day, and I love you more than words can express.

To the next generation of investors who use their financial freedom
to write their own stories and improve their corner of the world.

"

ACKNOWLEDGMENTS

I always talk about partners and teams and how they are integral to success. This book is no exception and would not have been possible if not for an incredible team supporting me along the way.

First and foremost, my wife, **Erica Schwartz**, for going along with all of my crazy ideas. In the midst of a global pandemic, I decided to write a book and she supported me, no questions asked. Thank you for believing in me, standing behind all of my wild endeavors, and taking such great care of our kids so that I could write, and write, and write some more.

This book would not have been nearly as fun and interesting had it not been for **Beverly West**, who coached me, encouraged me, argued with me and cheered me on the whole way through.

The initial inspiration for all of this came from **Robert Kiyosaki** and **Lin-Manuel Miranda** whose insightful words at just the right moment, gave me a fresh perspective and the motivation to "take my shot."

Thanks to the many great teachers and mentors who have helped me along my path, especially **Brad Sumrok**, **Rod Khleif**, **Russell Gray**, **Robert Helms**, as well as the Real Estate Faculty at Boston University.

A special thanks to my team of experts who were instrumental in the crafting of the book: attorney **Merrill Kaliser**, CPA **Jim Ross**, and mortgage experts **Anthony Golebiewski**, **Sean Daly**, and **Mathew Eshagoff**. You are all amazing.

A special shout out to my amazing in-laws, **Elwin** and **Cheryl Schwartz**, who provided valuable feedback on an early draft of the book and stepped in at vital times when both Erica and I were on deadlines and needed a hand with the kids. Also **David Morovitz**, **Steve Suh**, **Jim Pfeifer**, **Bhushan Vartak** and **Chris Rush** were crucial through the editing process of the manuscript.

Thank you to **Julie Broad** and the entire team at Book Launchers who helped with all aspects of the book from editing through launch.

Lastly, but maybe most importantly, I want to thank my superior team of Beta Readers. These people, from all different backgrounds and levels of real estate knowledge, were able to give me great feedback on places where the manuscript could use clarification, making it a more valuable resource for readers like you. I am eternally grateful to each and every one of you, **Jerry Ackman**, **Aaron Adler**, **Paul Bonomi**, **Rama Chunhu**, **JB Colletta**, **Janvrin Demler**, **Sean Donnelly**, **Mike Dworman**, **Art Fisher**, **Andrew Frye**, **Thomas Gagnon**, **Michael Harris**, **Kyla Hashmi**, **Johannes Hennche**, **Greg Hodgson**, **Steve Jacoby**, **Grey Lee**, **Joe Montanye**, **Sandra Picheny**, **James Reade**, **Jim Reardon**, **Dan Relihan**, **Ben Roth**, **Eric Schultz**, **Sandhya Seshadri**, **Chris Soignier**, **Jeff Talbott**, **Jeremy Villano**, **David Weinstock**, **Catherine West**, **Justin Wilson**, **Siva Yegnanarayanan**, **Carrie Young**, and **Bob Zhu**.

IMPORTANT
PLEASE READ

This book is **NOT** intended to be advice of any sort. **You should seek out the services of professionals who are experts in the fields of investment, legal, and accounting for advice.**

The author and publisher specifically disclaim any responsibility or any liability, loss, or risk, personal or otherwise, which is incurred as a consequence, directly or indirectly, of the use and application of any of the contents of this book.

There is no warranty for the completeness or accuracy of the information in this book. Any facts and figures are provided solely to illustrate underlying principles.

This book provides information that is believed to be accurate at the time of publication. Laws and regulations change over time and vary by location and particular circumstances. **Seek the services of professionals who can provide advice tailored to your specific situation.**

Throughout the book, many of the people's names and identifying characteristics have been changed.

HOW TO
CONNECT WITH ME
ABOUT PASSIVE INVESTMENTS

I love chatting with people about passive investing. Whether you've never made an investment before or you're a seasoned pro, I encourage you to reach out to me to see if we can make any sparks fly.

Email:

matt@picheny.com

The best way to reach out to me for a one-on-one dialogue.

Website:

picheny.com

I regularly post videos and articles that I write on the website and you can join our Investors Club there.

The Backstage Briefing:

My monthly newsletter is a fantastic resource that provides investing tips, project updates, and educational content. Signup via the website.

SCAN HERE!

CONTENTS

MY ADVENTURES IN REAL ESTATE INVESTMENT

How would you like to achieve financial freedom while making the world a better place?

Passive real estate investment—investing without major hands-on participation—can be lucrative if you know what you're doing. It can help you improve life for yourself, your family, your community, and leave your corner of the world a little better than you found it.

I started out as almost an accidental investor. I stumbled my way into success through trial and error, by making good deals and bad, and by living with the rewards and the consequences of my decisions. I wrote this book to share what I've learned so that you can avoid some of the growing pains I've endured on my path to financial freedom. I'll go over the technical stuff you need to know, as well as some bigger lessons—like what my values are, what's important to me in a deal, and what success really means to me and why.

This book is intended for enlightened professionals from all walks of life—busy entrepreneurs, educators, doctors, managers, marketers—truly anyone who is interested in creating passive real estate income. It's a guide for everyone who enjoys their job and their busy life and would like to have a second income, but doesn't necessarily have the time to investigate all the ins and outs of how to achieve this.

Realizing that I could literally make money while I slept was a total game changer for me. It's extraordinary to watch your wealth grow and effect positive change in the world while you are busy doing other things. This kind of financial freedom is a very different concept than just being free of debt. This is the kind of freedom that invites new opportunities, new choices, and new results.

Real estate appeals to many as an investment opportunity because it's a tangible asset that's been used successfully to create wealth since practically the dawn of time. And let's not forget, there can be tremendous tax benefits available with real estate investment too. But unless you're a research-and-development nut like me, you probably don't have the time to cultivate in-depth knowledge about how to evaluate deals and determine if something is a wise investment or a situation you should turn and run away from—and quickly. So, many people avoid investing altogether, which is unfortunate.

In this book, I'll guide you through the highlights and lowlights of my adventures in real estate, from my start as a rank amateur leaving the acting world, all the way up to where I am now: an investor in thousands of apartment units across the country and even a few hit Broadway shows (yes, they can be rewarding passive investments, too).

Did I get rich quick in real estate? No, I did not. But I am now in the position to make my own decisions about how I spend my time, whether it's on business, on Broadway, or watching my daughter graduate from kindergarten. I can be where I want to be, when I want or need to be there. I have to say, it's a wonderful life.

There is no way I can teach you everything you need to know about passive investment in one book, or 10 books for that matter; I could wallpaper a small state with my spreadsheets alone. And some things you just have to learn through personal experience. My purpose here is to lay a solid foundation for you, so that when you are looking at a deal, you'll understand it well enough to be able to ask the right questions, spot the warning signs that something might not be on the up and up, and avoid falling down some of the rabbit holes that I did.

I now own and operate an investment company. I talk to investors about opportunities—and people ask me to evaluate deals for them—every single day. This book contains answers to the questions I get asked most often, and offers information that I think will be of the greatest benefit to the kinds of investors who look to me for guidance.

The first thing I tell everyone is that many people are rushing into the passive investment world these days, especially when it comes to syndicated real estate deals. To be frank, a lot of these folks don't know what they're doing. There are also experienced people out there who are doing deals that are way riskier than anything I would want to be involved with. What can I say? I'm a cautious guy. I wouldn't say I'm risk averse exactly, but I like all my ends tied up neatly, I read the fine print in my contracts, and I don't like to be rushed. Ultimately, I like to do deals where everybody involved walks away happy. So let's just say, I'm picky.

Many successful people—yours truly, for example—have started their careers by becoming involved in real estate while working another 9-to-5 job. Later, they decide they want to quit their day job and do this full-time and there's absolutely nothing wrong with that. But if you and your family are going to be dependent on real estate investments to replace the income that was once provided by a steady job, you might want to move gradually toward total commitment. Real estate is like showbiz; it can be unpredictable even after you get the hang of things. If someone needs to do deals and collect fees in order to put food on the table—if someone's livelihood depends on those fees—they might be tempted to start doing deals that they might not do if they were in a position to pick and choose. You don't want to put yourself in that position, or to get involved in deals that are underwritten by people in that situation either.

Desperation usually demands making compromises. The real estate market is continually growing more competitive. Deals and margins get tighter and tighter. To have a deal work on paper, sometimes you have to be a little less conservative with some of your calculations; I've seen deals become complicated with people I've respected and have invested with in the past but who've started getting aggressive with their underwriting.

If someone can substantiate what they're doing, I don't have a problem with that. But I fear that more and more people are underwriting deals in a manner that cannot withstand any shocks to the economy. If things continue to go up and up and there are bright sunny skies and smooth sailing as far as the eye can see, then those people have a potential to make a lot of money for themselves and their investors. But at the first sign of a storm, they are going to be in really big trouble. I try to avoid those types of deals and, hopefully, with the use of this book, you can avoid them too.

I've earmarked things you need to look out for and question, and, on the flip side, I point out signs that a deal is solid gold. But more than that, I hope to have conveyed a bigger picture that will help you to consider real estate investment in a new way. Because real estate investing can be a new kind of activism, allowing you to effect change where you see it's needed and improving life for others—and the planet—by putting your money to work in the world in a way where everybody can benefit. My deals are always win-win and about more than the bottom line. For this reason, I do not underwrite aggressively. Instead, I look for deals where everybody wins, where properties are improved and greened, where my investors make money, the residents who live in my properties enjoy a better quality of life, and the planet is a little better off too.

What follows is my story in passive real estate investment. Yours will be different, reflecting your priorities, preferences, goals, and purpose.

Are you ready to begin your journey to financial freedom?

Good. Let's get started.

Matt Picheny

CHAPTER 1

NEW BEGINNINGS

O n a beautiful Sunday morning in June 2015 my wife, Erica, and I were at our rental house at Woodridge Lake in northwest Connecticut, getting it ready for the summer. We had to leave in a few hours to make sure we made it back to our place in Brooklyn in plenty of time to watch the Tony Awards on TV that night. Usually we would have gone to some of the award festivities in person, but we were taking it easy that year and staying home with our daughter who wasn't even a year old at the time.

"I just got a strange email," Erica said with a funny smile on her face. "Of course, I would never do it."

"Do what?" I asked.

"Someone just reached out to me about a job in Miami."

"Miami?"

"Yeah, crazy," Erica said with a giggle and shook her head.

My wheels immediately started spinning. We were living in our townhome in Brooklyn, a duplex we had purchased and renovated just over a year before. Erica has since told me she thought it was going to be our "forever home," and while I hadn't thought of living there forever, I certainly hadn't planned on leaving so soon after finishing all the work on the place.

Plus, I mean, it was Miami. I had grown up in Orlando, so I was very familiar with Florida, but I had never been a Miami fan. It was hardwired into us Orlando folks—while I appreciated the cultural atmosphere of Miami, it was a "party town" and no place to settle down with a young family. No way we were moving there.

Over the course of the next few weeks though, Erica and I both realized this opportunity could be a real game changer for her. She worked on the business side of the theater world in New York City and had deep roots in the business of Broadway. People might think Broadway shows are run by large corporations since they're at the top of the food chain when it comes to live performance but most of the shows are actually run by very small companies.

The opportunity in Miami, on the other hand, would give Erica the chance to work at a very large performing arts center, The Adrienne Arsht Center. It was a chance to expand her experience beyond her career with Broadway shows and an opportunity to lead a large team. She would be responsible for the programming and operations of multiple performance spaces with not only Broadway shows but also live music, dance, and comedy. I was beginning to see that I might have to reassess my feelings about Miami for Erica's sake.

Erica made the final cut for the gig in Miami. Of course she did—I couldn't imagine it turning out any other way. My wife is a born leader. The performing arts center flew her to Miami for the final round of interviews;

it was down to her and one other candidate. They wined and dined her, gave her a tour of the theaters, and she got great seats for the production that was running at the time. She came back to our home in Brooklyn as effervescent as champagne. I knew right then that Erica and I, with our one-year-old daughter, were moving to Miami.

Looking back on my life, I realize there have been pivotal moments like this that have led me to where I am today. As you will see, my path to financial freedom has been quite unique. I wasn't born with a silver spoon in my mouth and I didn't even go to a traditional college. Consequently, this book is not a traditional A to Z on how to become a gazillionaire in the amazing world of real estate investing. I'm not going to sell you a course on how to think rich and prosper. Instead, this is the story of how I have navigated the labyrinth of real estate investing—what happened to me along the way, and the way it's turned out so far.

In this story, you'll meet all sorts of characters—both good and bad—and I'll share with you many of the lessons I learned about real estate investment, and about life. All of them are true stories, although I may have changed some names and circumstances to protect people's anonymity. I'll offer some practical and actionable lessons that you can put to good use in your own real estate investing journey.

I've laid out the story chronologically, but since real estate deals can span many years and some lessons build upon earlier teachings, there are occasional jumps in the timeline. The dates are not the important things. The important parts are the takeaways from the story, so don't get too bogged down on exactly when they happened.

Ultimately, I think you will see that this hasn't been an easy road, but I will tell you that once you approach the summit of the mountain of financial freedom...well, all I can say is, the view from here is spectacular. Now back to my transformative moment.

You have to be able to go where you need to go, when you need to go there

"Erica, you have to take this job," I said. She nodded excitedly. As much as we both loved New York and our new home in Brooklyn, this was just too good an opportunity for her to pass up. I was less certain about my own prospects down south, but I certainly wasn't going to stand in Erica's way.

I jumped into project manager mode and researched apartment rents and the cost of living differences between Brooklyn and Miami. I entered all of this information into a spreadsheet, added up the costs involved with the move, and calculated the bottom-line number that Erica would need to earn in order for us to make the move and live in Miami until I found a job there. There was no assurance if, or when, I'd be able to find a job that would replace the kind of salary I was making in New York City. We wouldn't have the same quality of life we had in New York right away of course, but even if we had to live on PB&Js and popcorn for a while, I needed to know that we could carry the subsistence costs—pay rent, utilities and feed ourselves.

I came up with a number. Erica's offer came in a little under that number, but we had some savings and a couple of small investments and this was such a great opportunity for Erica's career, we figured we could make it work.

Don't burn the bridge, bridge the distance instead

Long ago, I learned to keep bridges intact and all my options open—just in case. I figured I'd need safety nets if I ever took a flying leap into the unknown. As it turned out, that was a good call, at least at the onset. Knowing there are options helps me feel more relaxed about things, and relaxation is the key to smooth take offs and safe landings.

I let my team at work know what was happening. I worked at a large advertising agency in New York City and they were in talks to acquire a small agency in Miami, so there was a chance I could slide in there. Not yet, though. I would need to wait and see. That didn't sound too solid to me, so I didn't rely on it, but it was good to have at least one iron in the fire.

For caution's sake, we decided we would rent a place instead of buying for at least the first year. It was important to us to hang onto our past while stretching into an uncertain future, so we wanted to hold on to our Brooklyn property in case we came back. We also knew that we could rent out our home for more money than our expenses, which would provide us with positive **cash flow** while I looked for work.

Backstage Glossary

Cash Flow: The movement of money. Positive cash flow is profit that you have after you've received income from an asset and paid for all of its expenses.

Everything was still very uncertain where Florida was concerned. The only thing we knew for sure was where Erica's job would be. We didn't have a lot of friends there and weren't familiar with any of the neighborhoods. Should we live in Miami Beach, which we learned is actually an island, or should we live on the mainland? Was this transition really going to work? Would I find work? Would my old job come through? We had no idea about any of these things.

Erica had a college friend, Greg, who had put down roots in Miami and owned a home there. Greg knew quite a bit about the area and didn't seem to mind helping us out, so we started barraging him with questions.

Erica and I flew down and spent a few days in Miami about two months prior to our move. It was a bit of a bumpy ride, looking at rentals with a very eccentric real estate agent who didn't inspire much confidence. But after a couple of days, we settled on an apartment in a building on a small island in between the mainland and Miami Beach.

The apartment was a two-bedroom with a den that would make a great room for our baby daughter. It was a cozy (read tiny) place, but it gave us amazing views of the beach to the left and the mainland to the right, from our living room. At night it looked like a lit-up wonderland on the water. We knew this was the place for us. No square footage, but loads of charm.

When you find what you're looking for, jump on it

There was a lesson in this experience that has proven true many times since: when you see something that is perfect for you, jump on it. Don't wait. Don't hesitate when it comes to great investments or you could very well lose out.

Erica and I already knew from our experience with New York real estate that if you blink your eyes, a place can vanish. We filled out the paperwork for the apartment on the spot and had funds ready to go. But that's when I learned the hard way that sometimes, even when you're primed and prepared, you can still lose out on a property, especially if your agent isn't as agile or motivated as you are. This was the moment when the importance of good partnerships came home to me, big time.

After a few weeks of constantly following up with the real estate agent, he somehow managed to bungle the transaction and we lost the apartment just before we were due to move. Catastrophe! Now we not only needed a new place to live, but we definitely needed a new real estate agent.

We reached out to yet another questionable agent who told us that in all of Miami, there was only one house that fit our criteria. As our good fortune would have it (and I figured at that point that karma owed us one), that house was just a few blocks away from where Erica's friend Greg lived. We asked him to look at it for us since another trip to Florida before the move was impossible. Greg shot a video for us on his phone, gave us the thumbs up, we signed the lease, and moved into the house a week later.

The place was livable. It wasn't a shotgun shack but it wasn't in great shape either. Most importantly though, it was available and fit our modest budget. We spent several weeks trying to spruce up the place with curtains and other small improvements that made a bit of a difference, but we knew we'd be looking for new digs once I found a job.

We made the move in September of 2015, and for the remainder of that year I met with advertising agencies in the area in search of a full-time job. I got great feedback from each of them, but never found the right fit. It was an odd experience for me. For the previous 18 years in New York, I was constantly being recruited out of one agency and into another, working on larger and larger teams.

Part of the problem for me was that the agencies in Miami were much smaller than I was used to. In New York, I managed global teams of 100+ people, whereas in Miami, an entire agency would have 10 to maybe 30 people. I received a couple of offers but they weren't exciting roles and I was stunned at how low the salaries were. The scale was completely different on every level, and the jobs just didn't seem worth the enormous sacrifice of time and energy that I knew from experience ad agencies always demand.

To be honest, I was burned out! I was 42 years old, and for nearly two decades I had worked long hours, putting in weekends in the office and all-nighters when campaigns launched. My hard work had caused me to miss important moments with my family. If I were going to do that again, there'd have to be a large number at the end of the offer, and that wasn't happening in Miami.

I decided I needed a new life plan. This was a frightening but important pivot point for me. I had started heading in the direction of freedom, but in the beginning it didn't feel like that at all.

Passive income dreams

While all of this was going on, I had extra time on my hands and decided to listen to audio books that could help round out my financial knowledge. Up to that point, I had made a few investments, mostly by instinct, not really knowing consciously what I was doing or why. I certainly didn't have a "system" yet. I thought a little guidance might be helpful.

I had heard of *Rich Dad, Poor Dad* by Robert Kiyosaki, so when the title came up, I chose his audiobook. His words were powerful. They really shifted my mindset. The biggest takeaway for me was that I needed to create multiple streams of **passive income** that would combine to create critical mass and, ultimately, financial freedom. This meant a diversified portfolio that I could manage without having to work myself to death.

Backstage Glossary

Passive Income: Money that comes to you with no effort on your part. It may take a small amount of effort to set up but virtually none to maintain. You can literally make money while you sleep. Examples are rental income or the income from business activities in which you do not materially participate.

If I had lots of little streams of income that were completely passive—I didn't have to do anything for them—then once I had enough of them, I would never have to work. I wouldn't need to trade my time for money ever again. Of course, I would still work on the things I wanted to, but I would never be beholden to a company or person ever again. This would allow me to spend time with the most important things to me—my family leading the list. Passive income would mean I wouldn't have to miss milestones in my daughter's life because I had to work. I really liked the sound of that!

KEYSTONE CONCEPT #1
Don't Trade Your Time for Money

They say time is money, but actually, time is more valuable than money. You can always find ways to generate more money. You can't generate more time. Instead of working for money, have your money work for you. Once you have enough passive income, you don't have to trade your time for money.

I began to understand that passive income streams are of paramount importance when it comes to financial freedom. I looked at where I was and was pleased to discover that I already had a couple of relatively successful passive income streams that were really helping with this sudden move to Miami.

The first was our two-family townhome in Brooklyn. Tenants lived on the top floor and we had lived on the ground floor, so when we moved to Miami we rented out our unit too. The rental income from those two apartments paid for all of our monthly expenses (including the mortgage) with a nice little surplus. And then, of course, there was *Hamilton*! Yes, I do mean THE *Hamilton*….

We had invested in the Broadway production of *Hamilton*. We loved the show, having seen it performed downtown at the Public Theater before it moved to Broadway. We were fortunate enough to have been able to invest a small amount in it, thanks mainly to my wife. (I told you Erica was a mover and a shaker.) But while we believed the show would be a big success, we didn't realize it would become such a phenomenon.

It was yet another moment in my life when I learned, very much like Hamilton did, that when opportunity appears, you have to seize it.

Don't throw away your shot

Miami was a strange new place. I was going on agency interviews for jobs that I was not interested in and that didn't pay well, while at the same time being totally burned out on agency life. Meanwhile, I was listening to Kiyosaki talk about building passive income and, whenever I needed a break, listening to the *Hamilton* cast album. That show was on a constant loop in our household. I was still pursuing my safe and sensible approach to life, but was yearning for something more. I was still trying to straddle both worlds, struggling to keep all options open, and boy was I getting tired.

One afternoon, after another session of *Rich Dad Poor Dad*, I switched over to the *Hamilton* cast recording. The moment I heard the words, "I am not throwing away my shot!" in the final verse of "My Shot," I had an epiphany: *What the hell am I doing here?* I asked myself. *Why am I killing myself trying to find a job that I don't even really want? Why am I fighting to get into the rat race that most people are trying to escape? Why did I want to go back to that? Why was I throwing away my shot to do something I love?*

It seemed my stars had aligned in the real estate arena, which was something I'd subconsciously pursued—I always had a property I was working on, no matter how busy I was in my advertising jobs. I'd even built a lake house from scratch in my down time. Of course real estate was where I should be, I realized. This was my shot. It had been right under my nose the whole time.

I talked with Erica about what I was thinking, explaining that I wanted to focus on real estate full time and hopefully develop some good, solid, passive income streams. I also told her I knew that as a rank amateur we would have to rely on her job as our only stable stream of income for the first years—who knew how many.

We talked about the fact that we already had two streams of passive income and maybe the rental house at the lake would eventually turn a profit. Over time, I could build up multiple streams of income through multiple investments. I wasn't exactly sure how this was going to go down, but I knew I could do it, or at least I knew that I wanted to try. The business of straddling both worlds had to go. I needed to focus my energy where it belonged.

In retrospect, it sounds pretty crazy, charting into the unknown with a wife and one-year-old daughter and without a secure salary. I know now that it was the right move, but I didn't know that for sure back then.

How did I have the confidence to take on such a monumental risk? I'd had previous encounters in my life when I faced what seemed impossible. I knew that when things felt hopeless, I'd dug in deep, taught myself new skills, figured out new options, picked myself up by my bootstraps, and powered through. It's what led me to the place I was now, with a few resources, a little money in the bank, and a couple of cash flowing assets. I remembered the first time this happened. That dark time back in 2001 when I thought all was lost. Back when I had nothing.

RENT

" **Y**ou've got 90 days to get out!"

"Wait, what?"

Panic set in. Where was I going to live? I don't think my landlord cared about that, and he wasn't some slumlord with evil intent yelling at me through the cigar poking out of the side of his mouth either. He was a relative.

After the adrenaline wore off, I realized he had broken it to me in the nicest way possible. It was 2001 and the dot-com bubble had burst, sending financial markets into a tailspin, and this was *before* the World Trade Center came down. 2001 was quite a year in retrospect.

I understand now that my relative had financial obligations and the time had come for him to sell the **co-op** apartment he owned and that I had been lucky enough to live in. After all, this was valuable real estate in the heart of Chelsea, a great neighborhood in New York City where I never could have afforded to live without his generosity.

> **Backstage Glossary**
>
> **Co-op:** A multi-unit building that is owned collectively by all the owners. While all the units are owned co-operatively, each unit has its own proprietary lease assigned to a particular owner. Co-ops have bylaws and are controlled by a co-op board consisting of elected members. They have maintenance fees that are paid by members to cover the property's expenses, including property tax.

When I moved into that apartment, I was a poor, starving actor. My total income for the entire year was $7,891. This co-op had been a dream come true, and I made a lot of dreams come true while living there. Now it was time to wake up and face real Manhattan rent prices. It was time to move on. I had to admit that the co-op and I had a good run, but back then, I was really scared to leave it behind.

Manhattan or bust

I grew up in Orlando, Florida in the '70s and moved to New York in 1992 to pursue a career in theater. I had caught the performing bug early in life. I'm told my first performance playing a bird in a preschool play brought the house down. Check out the photo of me in front of our apartment on my first day of preschool in my groovy threads. I look like I belong in an episode of *Starsky and Hutch*—clearly born for stardom. What got me hooked on the theater for real was my breakout performance playing the male lead in my fifth grade production of *Mary Poppins*. I got rave reviews.

By the age of 12, I was singing and dancing up a storm with Mickey Mouse in front of the castle at Disney World. Things just seemed to proceed kind of magically from there, as things have a tendency to do in the Magic Kingdom.

Matt Picheny at Oakwood Village, 1976

Matt at Age 16, smiling and performing at Disney World as Mowgli from The Jungle Book.

As the picture clearly foreshadows, I was Broadway bound. I moved to New York City to attend The American Musical and Dramatic Academy (AMDA). It was exhilarating, spending my days absorbed in my craft and waiting in line for hours to get cheap seats to see Broadway shows. I did pretty well at first, which I'm told is rare among my kind. I was going out on auditions, getting callbacks, and actually booking gigs. And this time I wasn't in a flesh-colored leotard and I ditched the wig. Check out my head-shot. New York was polishing me, like a rock in a tumbler.

Mathew Jason Picheny

Matt's headshot, 1993

One look at this picture and you can see why I got scooped up in a hot second: I look like I'm 12. I could play any kid in any show on Broadway, but as an adult I didn't come with the restrictive union regulations that child actors do. I was casting director candy. I booked my first show out of New York while still in my final semester at AMDA. Three days after graduation, I was off on a tour, performing around the country. I had officially become what every actor must at some point become—homeless.

Put down roots that will endure over time

Ironically, it was touring that taught me how much I really wanted to put down roots. I realized that I'm not a gypsy at heart. I needed a roof over my head, some real walls, and a bed that wasn't on wheels. So, when the nine-month tour was over, I rented a small apartment with a roommate in some hellscape near Harlem. The sidewalks didn't so much sparkle as crunch with discarded crack vials.

It was after my roommate had been mugged twice in our neighborhood that I made the decision to take up my relative's generous offer to live in his co-op in exchange for taking over the maintenance payments. When I moved into Chelsea in 1996, I felt like I was home, and I needed a home badly. I put down roots, and as soon as I did, I began to grow in a new direction. I was learning what it really meant to be a New Yorker. And I was learning what real estate meant to me on a fundamental and personal level. All extremely useful lifelong lessons.

During the five years that I was a working actor in New York, I was in 15 productions. I earned membership in the Actor's Equity union, performed in every major city in the continental United States, worked at regional theaters coast-to-coast, and even worked off-Broadway. I performed in shows like The Who's *Tommy*, and *The Fantasticks* at regional theaters. I did *Oliver!* at The Paper Mill Playhouse and *Finian's Rainbow* at The Goodspeed Opera house, two of the most prestigious theaters in the country.

What did *Oliver!* and *The Fantasticks* have to teach me about real estate investment? Actually, quite a bit. Being an actor made me a well-rounded person. I knew I had what it took to pursue a dream, face rejection, and land on my feet like a cat no matter what happened. Those are good things to know as an entrepreneur. I also learned a lot about business and marketing because, as an actor, you have to learn how to market the hardest product to sell in the world—yourself.

Thanks to my stature and my baby face, I was able to pick up an astonishing amount of acting work. But much to my surprise and horror, I wasn't the only adult who could play juvenile roles. There were quite a few of us, so I have to attribute my success to the attention I paid to the business aspects of show business. As I'd heard so many times, "business" is the larger of the two words.

I treated my career with the same respect, diligence, and persistence that any good business owner would. I trained with the best coaches in town and went to every possible audition. Even if there wasn't a role for me in a show, I'd be up before dawn for cattle call auditions. I'd stand in line for hours (often in the freezing cold and brutal NYC wind) with hundreds of other hopefuls outside the Actors' Equity Building in Times Square to get my chance to sing 16 bars (about 40 seconds) of a song that would inevitably be followed with an audibly unenthusiastic, "next."

At each audition, I'd take down the names of all the people in the room who were evaluating me. I'd also write down what song (or sometimes songs if I was lucky) I sang and exactly what clothes I was wearing. I did this because, if I got a callback (a chance to continue in the audition process at a later date), I wanted to be able to wear the same outfit and sing the same song(s). I went on a lot of auditions in those days—usually two to four per day—which made it difficult to remember what I'd worn or sung at any particular audition. To keep track, I drew a grid on a piece of paper, like a spreadsheet, and wrote everything down.

I figured it was probably hard for the people in the room to remember everyone who auditioned as well. By singing the same songs and wearing the same clothes at a callback, I thought it might help them to remember why it was they liked me to begin with. After every audition I would follow up with a postcard (that had my headshot on it) thanking them for their time.

That postcard was what got me my first show after graduation. I was told by the director of that show that I had made it through the auditions and was one of the final few people being considered, but they cast someone else in the role. They offered him the role but he turned it down and that very same day my postcard arrived in the mail, so they gave me the opportunity.

KEYSTONE CONCEPT #2

Be Persistent

Julie Andrews is attributed with saying: "Perseverance is failing 19 times and succeeding the 20th." Or as Captain Taggart says in *Galaxy Quest:* "Never give up, never surrender!"

Pretty cool coincidence, huh? It wasn't the first time something like that happened. When I was 12, I joined my sister, Melissa, at an audition to work at Disney World. It was massive, at a huge convention center, with hundreds of kids like us all wanting to be a part of the dream. Melissa really wanted to audition, I was just sort of along for the ride. A lot of her friends from dance school were there among what seemed like a million girls. There was just a handful of guys. I ended up getting a callback and getting cast in the show. Melissa didn't get cast in the show but I take my hat off to her for taking the news so well. I'm sure that must have stung a bit.

Before the audition, I had been told by everyone to keep a smile on my face because they like smiles at Disney. As the team was trying to determine who would be cast, each time they looked at me throughout the entire day, I was sitting there with an ear-to-ear grin. Truth be told, I thought my cheeks were going to fall off that day. In fact, they were sore for hours after all of that smiling. Every time they looked my way, a big smile from Matt.

After I got the Disney show, my father had a conversation with the director during rehearsals one day. The director told my dad I had the skills to do the show but there were a couple of other kids who were just as good. But there I was with that ridiculous smile. All. Day. Long. The director said he could see that I wanted it badly and that I worked so hard to keep smiling that they knew I would give it my all. It seemed to mean so much to me. So, they gave me the job. That's a lesson in persistence that I've never forgotten. It's also a lesson in the power of a smile.

Here's another story about persistence. I had always loved music and rock was my passion until high school, when I got into the alternative thing. I was listening to bands like U2, The Cure, and R.E.M. before they went mainstream. Just after I graduated, Nirvana released their album *Nevermind*, which officially welcomed the "grunge" scene into the spotlight of American youth culture.

Truth be told, I really wanted to be a rock/alternative musician but I lacked that whole vibe. I enjoyed singing and playing my guitar but was never much of a songwriter and I wasn't in a band. (Well, there was that short-lived trio in my garage in high school, but we were absolutely terrible.) So musicals are where I ended up. I had grown up with some exposure to them and performed in a few in community theaters and at school. I really enjoyed the more contemporary shows like *Rent*, and my favorite professional role was when I was in a production of The Who's *Tommy*.

My fellow performers had CDs of Andrew Lloyd Webber and Stephen Sondheim, while mine were the Beatles and Nirvana. When I was at AMDA, I realized I would probably not be working full-time as an actor when I graduated and would likely need to wait tables between gigs. I thought the Hard Rock Café would be a great place to work: the original Hard Rock location on 57ᵗʰ Street was not too far from the theater district and I would be surrounded by awesome music. The place was perpetually busy, and as a result it was notoriously competitive. It was nearly impossible to get a job there, but I refused to accept defeat!

My original inquiries there were futile, but after months of persistence, I found out that the guy I needed to talk to was a manager named Keith, who looked like a rock star himself. I remember the first time I saw him on the floor, standing on a raised platform, looking beyond cool with his arms crossed, monitoring everything going on under his watchful eye like a Hard Rock God.

Somehow, I found the nerve to chat with Keith and we hit it off. We bonded over our love of music and that we both played guitar. He told me he didn't have anything for me at that time but to check back in a little while. I told him I really wanted the job, that I was a hard worker, and that I would casually swing by every Thursday at 4 p.m. until he gave me a chance. I did that for two months, every Thursday. And finally, one day, one of Keith's food runners was sick and he asked me to come in on Friday to try it out. It worked out well and I started as a food runner. I ended up working at the Hard Rock for the rest of AMDA and for many years after. Over time, I trained in every role possible, including host, merchandise sales, busboy, and, finally, the coveted "server" role.

So there I was, working at the Hard Rock after another out-of-state show. I felt like I had paid my dues and was waiting to be cast in a Broadway show. I was tired of bus and truck tours. My plan was to keep waiting on tables and keep smiling until I got a Broadway show.

Matt picking the pockets of George S. Irving's Fagin in the
1994 production of Oliver at the Papermill Playhouse

Master the tools of progress

As a guy who has benefitted enormously from tools of all kinds, I have
learned on my unlikely journey that it's important to keep your skills up-to-
date and master the tools that you are going to need to make progress. You
have to be ready and willing to learn new things, master new techniques,

try out new tools, and access the technology of progress. Hang back and you'll get left in the dust, no matter what you choose to do in life.

During my last show on the road, I bought my first laptop computer. I had expressed an interest in getting one and my mother said she would help me pay for it on the condition that, when I got back to NYC, I would look into getting some sort of computer-based job to work in between acting gigs instead of waiting tables. My mother was pretty smart about things like that. She pointed me in a direction I didn't realize I wanted to go. Fortunately, my mom knew exactly what she was doing.

I half-heartedly agreed but, truthfully, I wanted the computer so I could communicate with my friends through America Online (AOL). For those of you for whom the last century is already ancient history, having an AOL account was all the rage at that time. It was one of the only ways to do this miraculous new thing called "logging on to the Internet."

You would plug your computer into a phone jack and click on a button on your screen to sign-in. After a few minutes of audible static, clicks, chirps, beeps, and other otherworldly sounds, you would be greeted with a fabulous fellow saying "Welcome" followed with a possible "You've Got Mail" if you had gotten lucky and someone had sent you email since the last time you logged in. This was revolutionary. You could send email, or even better, instant messages to your friends and they would respond in real time! It's hard to capture in words how truly exciting the Internet was to experience back then.

One evening, I received an email from my friend David, and it had a hyperlink in it. I had never seen anything like that before. I clicked on the link and—lo and behold!—David's headshot and résumé miraculously appeared on my screen. This was nothing short of mind-blowing! I saw this as a fantastic marketing tool and the nerd inside me thought it was oh so cool.

I started creating my own online headshot and resume and noticed a button on the menu for the website building program that read "HTML." When I clicked on that button, the entire screen turned from the webpage I was making into some strange text-only version with a bunch of letters and characters. I started to realize that as I made changes in the visual editor, changes would happen in the HTML version. I started to learn the connection between the two, and within a few weeks, I wasn't using the visual editor anymore, I was building my pages using this language called HTML. I had become a coder.

I made my "website" much more interactive than David's had been. I put my newly discovered, super cool, totally nerdy hyperlinks on each show on my resume and linked them to photos from the production. I showed my work to my parents, who were very impressed. It turned out that my dad had a one-page website for his business that someone had made for him and I offered to revise it for him for free.

Both of my parents were entrepreneurs. My dad had been involved in many different businesses from retail to real estate to the food service industry. My mother had started a roof consultancy business with a partner.

My mother saw the website I had built for my dad and told me her business had a web page that needed some work. Eager to encourage my new obsession, she offered me a couple hundred dollars to do that. Then I had a friend who was opening up a recording studio. He wanted a website and paid me to create it.

The next thing I knew, my childhood best friend's sister called me out of the blue. She was working for a "new media" company in the city and had heard I was building websites. She said I should come in and talk with her.

It didn't take long for me to realize that my digital hobby was paying off big time. It sure paid a lot more than the $200 a week I made on bus and truck tours or the tips I was getting at the Hard Rock. Also, I liked the work.

I found the same sort of fun and creative energy in those early dot-com agencies that I had found in the theater. Ad agencies in the city were packed with creatives who were mostly actors and musicians anyway.

I dove deep into developing my digital skills and had no social life. My best friend and roommate from AMDA, Len, says that I essentially locked myself in my apartment for a year and came out a computer genius. "Genius" is definitely an exaggeration, but I worked day and night to teach myself how the Internet works. I learned several programming languages and developed the ability to utilize specialized software applications. I scaled back my hours at the Hard Rock and eventually left.

My year-long deep-dive paid off. The work became too much for me to do during regular work hours, so I started working after-hours from home. Eventually, I worked from home all the time and new clients kept coming in.

I bought a second desk and computer and would hire other people to come to the apartment to help me out. I'd charge clients a slight mark-up on what I was paying my assistants and eked out a small profit there. Soon, I needed a third desk and I had officially outgrown my small apartment. I rented office space down the street, and before I knew it, and without really meaning to, I was now the head of my own boutique agency, Picheny Productions. We did everything from simple brochure websites to high-profile e-commerce applications and cutting-edge projects for that time: integrating technologies like Flash and Cold Fusion with databases that allowed us to get some pretty cool projects for clients like the New York Yankees, Arista Records, and the cable channel Showtime.

And it all happened because I accessed a new tool of progress in order to communicate with my friends.

Read the writing on the wall and do what it tells you

An important thing to remember is that you have to stay alert to the shifts in your sector and yourself. Don't get lulled into complacency by success or scared off by failure. Keep a steady pace, pay attention to changes in the wind, and adjust strategically as needed. You don't want to rock the boat, but don't sit tight while it sinks either.

I learned this lesson about listening to what your experience is telling you during my final years as an actor in NYC. The time had come when I had to admit that my life was headed in a different direction. My digital business had been doing great for a couple of years. Then one day, I got a phone call from a casting agent.

A phone call from a casting agent is something you hope and pray for as an emerging actor. They were calling to ask me to audition for a production of *Cinderella* that was going out on tour and was hopefully headed to Broadway. The show even had celebrity headliners Deborah Gibson and Eartha Kitt. It was the big break I had been waiting for.

I went in for what was probably the worst audition of my life. I got a callback but I knew it was out of courtesy and, of course, I never heard from them again. I realized that my audition was terrible because I was not in top shape. I hadn't been acting, singing, or dancing for a few years; I'd been too busy with my business. And you know what? I didn't mind. I was loving what I was doing. I enjoyed my business and was having a blast. Plus, I was actually making nice money.

I read the writing on the wall and I understood what my life was telling me. I realized that I wasn't performing anymore and I was completely fine with that. I loved my time as an actor and wouldn't trade those years for anything in the world, but I was enjoying my life as the head of a boutique digital agency in the city even more. I realized the actor's life wasn't for me now and actually hadn't been for a few years, I just hadn't had time to notice. And it all started with that stealthy pact I made with my mom to get a laptop.

Be a tree and learn to bend

Then one day in 2000, all of those techno-vapor dreams came tumbling down and the bubble burst. People finally figured out that the new technology and the business models growing up around it needed to be more than just cool—they needed to make money. Investors got nervous, start-ups folded, blue chips were back, and my life in the digital world changed completely. Clients were a lot harder to come by, and everybody was tossing nickels around like they were manhole covers.

I had to learn some hard lessons about flexibility and agility, two crucial business and life skills if you're going to keep pace with your own destiny. When your world drops out from under you is when you really learn what you are all about deep down. And this is a good thing to know.

After the bubble burst, most of my clients weren't spending money on digital efforts anymore and business was way down. This was the moment when my relative called and told me I needed to leave the apartment.

I had 90 days to reinvent myself. What was I going to do?

I began to think about where I wanted to live and how I wanted to live. As is my usual process, I looked at the problem 600 ways to Sunday. Maybe I would have to move back home to Orlando. Could I move my business down there and probably stay at my parent's house for a little while? Maybe. Then once my business picked up, I could get my own place.

I really wanted to stay in New York but how could I afford to pay rent? I was living my favorite musical, clinging to a location I couldn't afford. I started thinking about the musical *Rent*, a story that influenced me at the beginning of my life in the city. The show is about a bunch of young adults in New York City who are squatters in a building on the Lower East Side, a neighborhood that is becoming gentrified. The antagonist, Benny, used to be their friend. But then he changed, married rich, and bought the building they live in. Benny demands that his former friends pay him the back rent they owe for the last year or get out. Now I was in a similar position. How was I going to pay rent? Or maybe…could I afford to buy something in this overpriced city?

Roger, one of the lead characters in *Rent*, laments what has happened to their friend Benny and the ideals he once pursued. Benny threw away his character and his friendships when he became an owner, a landlord willing to toss his friends out to the street. I wondered, did ownership really have to be that way? Couldn't I, for example, buy something that was good for everybody, a place where I could live affordably, and where I could maybe build a recording studio that all of my musician friends and I could use for free? I could have affordable residential units on the upper floors as my friends built their dreams in New York. Maybe I could give landlords a better name.

I thought back to a few years prior when my sister told me her doctor was selling his apartment on the Upper West Side. I loved that neighborhood in Manhattan. That's the neighborhood I went to school in, where I first learned what it was like to live in this amazing city. It's still my favorite neighborhood to this day.

My sister had done some babysitting for this doctor and gotten to know the family pretty well. She said he was selling the apartment and I started to look into what it might cost to buy an apartment on the Upper West Side. It was, of course, far too expensive for me at that time. That exercise though, that push to seriously consider a purchase, gave me a peek into the world of New York real estate.

KEYSTONE CONCEPT #3
Learn to Pivot

From Florida to New York. From actor to boutique agency owner. No matter what curveballs life throws your way, stay light on your feet and be able to change your steps when the dance calls for it.

Whether I bought or rented, one thing was clear. I needed to get a job. Paying real rent in New York, or trying to qualify for a **mortgage** to buy a place, would require a real job with a real salary. It just so happened that I knew that one of my clients, the cable channel Showtime, was looking to hire someone. One of the main duties for this role would be to update the website that Showtime had hired my company to build for them. When I told them I was interested in the job, it was a no-brainer for all of us. Just a couple of weeks later, I started working there and got a nice, steady paycheck. Thus began my career working in the digital media/advertising world. Now, I could contemplate a move.

Backstage Glossary

Mortgage: A legal document where a lender gives money to a borrower in exchange for an interest in something of value, usually a property.

Look for the signs

Could I actually buy something in one of the most competitive and cut-throat real estate markets in the world? And if I did, could I be an enlightened landlord and survive? If you're going to be an investor, you have to learn how to recognize an up-and-comer when you see one. Even if it's just a primary residence, knowing how to recognize a neighborhood with promise, an area that is about to turn around, is a valuable skill that you can learn by reading just a few simple cues.

I remember when I started looking at rental options on the Upper West Side. From what I could see from the realty company windows, the rents in the area were too high for me. It's so much easier today to check out rental info online, but back then, nothing of any substance was online. You had to window shop.

I started pounding the pavement and checking out rents in other neighborhoods as well. I had helped my sister move to Washington Heights, which is much further north, almost at the very top of Manhattan. In the couple of years that she lived there, I noticed an upswing in that neighborhood and real estate prices were on the rise. A couple of new restaurants, a Starbucks on the corner, the neighborhood was improving. This interested me. Maybe Washington Heights was a neighborhood whose moment had arrived and that I could still afford.

One day, my sister saw a listing on a local bulletin board for a one-bedroom apartment in a co-op building in the area being sold by the owner. At $125,000 and no broker fee, it was a steal for Manhattan real estate, even if Washington Heights, as fantastic and vibrant a community as it is, stretches the definition of what most people think of as Manhattan. So while I wasn't too thrilled with the idea of a longer commute, my sister assured me it was worth it. I thought this might be a good opportunity, so I called my expert on just about everything—my dad.

For most of my life, my dad was in the food service industry. At the height of his career in that sector, he was the hot dog king of Orlando, and actually ran a commissary where all of the other vendors could purchase product and clean their carts to be in compliance with state regulations. My dad got into this business because he accidentally drove by the property one day and saw a "For Sale by Owner" sign. I remember that every time he spotted one of those signs, he would stop the car and write down the number to contact the owner.

My dad had been a residential real estate broker earlier. He kept up his real estate license and would do a few deals on the side as they presented themselves. When he called this particular owner, he found out that the guy wanted to sell the business. He did a little digging and saw that it was a potential gold mine. He bought it and turned it into a profitable business.

I was old enough at the time to understand these types of things, and my father taught me what he was doing as he built the business. Once in a while, I would work a hot dog cart in a choice location right outside a night club where I got to hear great music—like Pearl Jam in their infancy. I worked the graveyard shift, when everybody would pile out of the clubs hungry and buzzing and head straight for my hot dog stand.

I called my dad to discuss the apartment opportunity with him. There were no online mortgage calculators in those days, so he pulled out his trusty Hewlett Packard financial calculator and worked up the monthly mortgage payments for me.

It turned out that I could afford to buy the apartment in Washington Heights. In fact, I would save at least $500 per month vs renting an apartment on the Upper West Side. Not only would I save money this way but my monthly mortgage payments would slowly be paying down the amount I would owe the bank for the new apartment. They call this gaining more **equity** in the property. This made complete sense to me. I checked out the apartment, it looked good, and before I knew it I was ringing in the new year in my very first real estate purchase, an apartment of my very own in Manhattan. And, more importantly, I had a place to live, and all within 90 days!

> **Backstage Glossary**
>
> **Equity:** The value of a property minus the claims against it, such as a mortgage.

CHAPTER 2 LESSONS LEARNED

- Look for the signs, pay attention to your target markets, and notice when the early milestones of community improvement start appearing.

- Stay flexible and agile emotionally, psychologically, and professionally. Be willing and able to adjust to changing circumstances and don't take it personally, just adjust.

- When the universe speaks to you, shut up and listen.

- Keep pace with the technological advances in your field, and stay on top of the tools that will give you an edge over the competition.

- Don't be afraid to let your dreams grow and change right along with you. When you are on a journey of discovery, it's impossible to know exactly where you are headed. Stay open to the possibilities.

CHAPTER 3

FROM RENT TO RICHES

I remember the day I first learned the difference between an asset and a liability—an important and eye-opening day. It was in January of 2002, I was fresh off the purchase of my very first apartment, and a friend tried to tell me what I had acquired was not an asset at all, but rather, a liability. I struggled to understand how my brand new and fabulous investment was actually a liability when it was clearly an asset! Buying an apartment was a great investment. Everyone told me so. Even my dad.

I have since come to understand that, technically, the apartment *was* a **liability**. I had a mortgage that I was responsible for paying every month. I also had additional costs, such as property tax, maintenance, and utilities that were mandatory for the operation of the apartment. All of these expenses represented cash flowing out of my pocket.

Backstage Glossary

Liability: Something you owe money for. Think of it as ownership of anything that costs you money. Money that flows away from you.

On the other hand, an **asset** is something that produces income. For example, if I owned the apartment and was able to rent it at a price that was greater than all my expenses, then I would be making money—cash flowing into my pocket.

— **Backstage Glossary** —

Asset: A thing of value. Think of it as ownership of something that makes you money. Something that generates money that flows to you.

I didn't understand assets and liabilities at that time but I liked the fact that my monthly costs were lower for owning vs renting. And over time, I would be gaining equity in the property by paying down the mortgage. Though I firmly believed the property would go up in value eventually, I didn't buy it as an investment. I bought it because I was being tossed out of my cozy Chelsea apartment, I needed a place to live, and this was the least expensive option.

Buying my apartment turned out to be a good decision for me, but the concepts of liability vs asset and ownership vs renting are worth a closer look (and could spark a quarrel with your partner if you're not careful). Sometimes renting is better than owning. It depends on your particular situation.

Today, people would look at me as if I have three heads if I told them that I don't own my primary residence. I am a real estate investor with thousands of units in my portfolio, so why in the world wouldn't I own my home? The bottom line is that there are times when the numbers haven't made sense for my particular situation.

For instance, when we lived in Brookline, Massachusetts, if we had purchased a home that matched our living situation, I would have been looking at a hefty monthly cost after accounting for mortgage payments, property tax, and insurance. I would have had a large liability that I needed to pay every month for as long as I owned the property (or at least the first 30 years, until the mortgage was paid off). I would also have to pay for all the repairs and maintenance on the property during my ownership and hope that the home would be worth at least the same as we paid for it if and when we decided to sell it. Historically, over time, real estate prices have gone up, and Brookline is a highly desirable area, but who knows.

The rental market in Brookline wasn't quite as hot as the market to buy. I found a great home for my family with a monthly cost that was about 60% less than the cost to own. The very large sum of money that would have been a down payment to purchase a home, was instead invested in cash-flowing real estate that provided us with additional income. We didn't worry about property tax or property insurance (we had renter's insurance) and didn't have a mortgage. We had a yearly lease, but beyond that, we were free to go whenever we wanted.

A look at owning instead of renting

Renting:

- Flexibility—no commitment longer than 1 year
- Can cost less than purchasing (depending on your location)
- Not responsible for maintenance
- Usually can't make large changes to the property
- No equity gain nor tax benefits

Owning:

- Building equity/paying down debt with a portion of your monthly payments
- Tax benefits
- Longer term commitment (usually doesn't make financial sense under five years)
- Can cost more than renting (depending on your location)
- Ability to make changes to the property
- Responsible for covering the cost and coordinating maintenance

My situation in New York back in 2001 was different than the situation in Brookline. As we discussed in the last chapter, my monthly cost for that apartment was $500 per month less to own than to rent. The apartment was in the Washington Heights area of New York City, which is in upper-upper Manhattan. It used to take me about 45 minutes, using the express subway, to get to my office in midtown Manhattan. The extra $500 a month I was "saving" by not renting an apartment was more than enough for a lot of things, including taking cabs when I needed to travel back uptown at night. Friends would lovingly tease me about how I "lived in Canada" because it was so far north. I was okay with that. I knew that I was building something.

A little over two years later, I found out what I had been building. I sold my apartment, which had more than doubled in value, and moved into a much nicer one-bedroom in my neighborhood of choice, the Upper West Side of Manhattan. Now my work commute was only 15 minutes and my friends were all impressed with the new apartment—that I *owned*.

So, I learned how to size up a situation and make a conscious decision about whether ownership or renting a place was the wiser choice. The fact that I managed to catch a glimpse of what it was like to be an owner was a real stroke of luck that should not have happened so quickly for me in a place like New York City, let alone learning what it felt like to see my investment skyrocket in record time.

Make the impossible possible with a few minor upgrades

So, how did this happen? How did I see the value of my Washington Heights apartment more than double in value in two years?

I attribute this partially to the growth in the New York City rental market, as well as to the upgrading of the Washington Heights area and my ability to notice the signs of progress. I can also take credit for the improvements that I was able to make in the apartment and the building, which increased the property's value exponentially. This has been part of my secret sauce ever since. Put some money into improvements. Improving the quality of the building in simple ways not only enhances the quality of life for everybody who lives there, it also does amazing things for your property value.

The unit I purchased in Washington Heights was in desperate need of TLC. With a few minor cosmetic upgrades—a new paint job and filling the many surface cracks in the walls—the apartment was more desirable than when I had bought it. More importantly, the building looked very dated when I first moved in. I became friendly with some of the co-op board members and I started talking with them about this issue. I eventually was asked to be on a committee with a couple of board members to propose and ultimately oversee a renovation to the lobby and hallways. Once this renovation was completed, the building looked much nicer and much more expensive. And as it turned out, it was exactly that.

KEYSTONE CONCEPT #4
Add Value
Figure out how you can add value to both your asset and the community at large. Improving the property and the surrounding community helps increase the value of your asset. This can have a dramatic and positive impact on your bottom line and it makes you, as an investor, an asset to your corner of the world.

Double the value, quadruple the equity

Here's another neat trick I learned in Washington Heights. While the apartment's value doubled, my equity in the apartment more than quadrupled! Why? Because I purchased the property with **leverage**, which is just jargon for saying that I got a mortgage. You see, the value of the property doubled but I only had to spend 25% of the purchase price as a down payment on the property and got a mortgage for the rest.

> ### Backstage Glossary
>
> **Leverage:** Using borrowed money to increase the potential return of an investment.

Let's break that down a little further with some actual numbers.

The Power of Leverage
(How the math adds up)

I purchased the property for $125,000 but put down only $30,000 of my own money and borrowed $95,000 from the bank.

I sold the property for $255,000, paid the bank back which left me with $160,000, a $130,000 profit after accounting for my initial $30,000 investment.

Since I only used $30,000 of my money and walked away with an additional $130,000, I more than quadrupled my investment.

Note that this is a broad example for illustrative purposes. It doesn't account for more nuanced debits and credits such as debt paydown, financing costs, and tax implications.

My **ROI** of 433% was huge! I used that profit for a down payment for another apartment. When I moved into my new place on 76th street I thought—Wow! I just made an enormous amount of money! I love this real estate thing. I was hooked!

> ### Backstage Glossary
>
> **ROI:** Return On Investment is a measurement of how much profit is made over the entire lifetime of an investment. It does not take into account the length of time your money is invested.

Don't stop 'til you get enough

Now this is where things get tricky. I found a system that worked for me once, so now I was determined to try it again and test the limits of my new formula for instant success. This is a juncture when people who are new to the business can get into trouble because when you're successful once, it can go to your head and you fail to realize that lightning may not strike twice.

I knew that there had been a bit of luck involved with the broader real estate market. Washington Heights was an emerging market with property values rising rapidly. The Upper West Side was a far more established area, yet very desirable, and Manhattan's real estate market was booming. I thought maybe I could take this ride again.

So, just as I had done with my first apartment, I made improvements to the new apartment. My plan was to live there for four or five years, at which point it would double in value and then I would move into a two or three-bedroom apartment in the same area. I imagined I could just keep trading up every five years or so until I had the penthouse of my dreams.

I had a bit of luck getting my apartment on the Upper West Side. The real estate market was so hot in 2004, units were going under contract at the first showing, with many "all-cash" offers. All-cash offers are more appealing to a seller because they can close within days instead of waiting months for banks to process and approve a mortgage.

I searched for months and finally came upon a great property on 76th Street, blocks away from my old school. For this particular unit, the floor in the living room (which was the majority of the apartment) had major damage. There had been some sort of radiator leak that severely warped the hardwood flooring. It looked like a quarter pipe from a skateboard park! Unless the apartment was being bought by the Birdman of skateboarding, Tony Hawk, that floor would need replacement. Other than that, it was perfect. I was determined to buy the place.

The first showing was the Sunday of Labor Day weekend, a terrible time for a showing as most people escape the city for the long weekend. I went to the open house and didn't see any other buyers there. I told the broker I was interested and followed up that evening with an offer that was slightly discounted to account for the floor repair. I was told that my offer would be considered but that they had an open house scheduled for Tuesday evening and they wanted to see how that went.

I decided to go to that open house too. Why? Because I wanted to see how much competition there was. As fate would have it, there was a torrential downpour that evening— like nothing I've seen before or since. I remember walking down the street to the apartment in hurricane-like conditions. I arrived soaking wet and stayed at the open house for almost the entire scheduled time and not a single buyer showed up. The storm was my friend that night. I chatted with the broker and built up some rapport with him. The next day I was told that my offer was accepted!

The day before I closed on the sale of my first apartment, all my belongings were put into a moving truck and I spent the night on the couch of my close friends from AMDA, Len and Tanisha. The next morning, I went to the closing of the sale of the Washington Heights property and that afternoon, with the profits in hand from the sale of the first property, I was able to close on the new property. Later that afternoon, all of my belongings were delivered to my brand-new apartment.

Plan on things not going as planned

Of course, as I have discovered many times since, if things can go wrong, they will. Being a project manager by trade and by nature, I had reviewed the plan with the flooring company twice over. Then we went over it a third time. All my belongings would be put into the bedroom of the new apartment by the moving company. The flooring team would replace the floors in the rest of the unit on the first day, and then on day two they would move my stuff into the living room and replace the bedroom floor. Len and Tanisha graciously offered their couch for the three nights it would take for the closing and floor repairs. Then I could move in. Simple, succinct, manageable, right? What could go wrong? As it turned out, just about everything.

Now I know to plan on things not going as planned, but back then I was a pure novice with a naive belief in the power of my organizational skills. As a result, I ended up on my friends' couch for more than a week and in a dispute with the flooring company that went on for months. When the dust settled on that disagreement, I got a massive discount and my great new floor cost a fraction of the original price.

For the first few months, I lived out of boxes: my apartment was a construction zone with a small pathway from the door to my bed and an even smaller path to the bathroom. Along with the flooring, I had built-in units and crown molding installed. And when all of that work was complete, I personally installed new lighting and had the entire apartment painted. It was a long process but, once complete, the place looked fantastic. Goodbye Birdman Hawk, hello second successful New York real estate investment.

Matt's Apartment on Manhattan's Upper West Side. 2013

I lived in that apartment for many years and really loved it. Things were going great and I eventually left my job at Showtime for an exciting opportunity at the famed Ogilvy advertising agency. I got to know my neighbors and they suggested I should be on the co-op board. Being involved with the board had worked out pretty well in Washington Heights, so eventually I did join the board and remained on it for rest of my time in that building, serving in several capacities, including board president.

During my time there, we made several improvements to the property including a lobby renovation, hallway upgrades, and a large project where we removed the broken intercom system (a must-have in NYC apartments without a doorman) and replaced it with a video system. The property was gradually increasing in value with every improvement.

When you are sinking, don't let go of the boat

Then, in 2008, the Great Recession came along and dealt a devastating blow to the economy and especially the real estate market. I saw the value of my apartment sink back down to around the price I had purchased it for. It was back to where it had started but I wasn't "underwater" on the place—where I would owe more on the property's mortgage than I could actually sell the property for. Unfortunately, a lot of people were not as lucky as I was during this economic crisis and countless people lost their homes.

When I had purchased the Washington Heights property, my father told me something that I don't think I truly understood until the recession. He said, "You never lose money in real estate if you never have to sell." It's very simple, yet profound. The value of the property doesn't matter while you own it. It only matters when you go to sell it. In my case, whether the property was valued at $1 or $1,000,000 at that moment, it really didn't matter. What mattered was that I had a mortgage to pay. Fortunately, I had a good job that wasn't affected too much by the financial turmoil. As long as I made that mortgage payment, I still owned the property. If I couldn't pay the mortgage, I could be foreclosed on and lose the property, or I could sell it at a loss. So I paid the mortgage and held on to the property.

Real estate, like the rest of the economy, moves in cycles. While you may want to sell when the market is depressed, you need the ability to hold on to the property and wait until the market is back up again. It's certain that the markets will always go up, just as they always go down. The variables are how far up or down they go and the timing of those cycles. Predicting those variables? That's something even the best and brightest get wrong. So, you need to be able to carry the costs if necessary, and wait for better market conditions.

KEYSTONE CONCEPT #5

Cash Flow Is King

Only buy properties that generate positive cash flow. This gives you the resilience you will need to ride out the inevitable dips in market cycles. Always remember, you never lose money if you never have to sell.

Taking that wisdom from my father and experiencing it in real life shaped the core of my investment strategy. Over time I learned that I should buy properties that were self-sufficient, so the mortgage and expenses could always be paid and the properties never had to be sold. But I hadn't completely learned that lesson yet. I had another adventure in store before that would become clear.

CHAPTER 3 LESSONS LEARNED

- Be aware of the neighborhoods you are interested in, and watch for the signs of improvement.

- You can vastly increase the value of a property with relatively minor improvements and upgrades.

- Construction projects always take longer than expected. Always.

- You never lose money on real estate if you never have to sell.

CHAPTER 4

MATT'S FOLLY?

One day in 2005, only about a year after I had purchased the property on 76ᵗʰ Street, I up and decided to build a house in a lakeside community from scratch, without any prior experience in construction. It was a bold and unique undertaking, and in the end, worth every lesson I learned along the way. But I would not recommend trying this at home.

It all started with a website. Well...two, actually.

My college roommate, Len, and his wife, Tanisha, now had a daughter, and we would travel to Litchfield, Connecticut, for a weekend or two each summer. My first visit to Litchfield had actually been for Tanisha and Len's wedding. Tanisha's parents had a house there and we stayed with them whenever we visited. It felt great to head up to "the country" for a few days to commune with a few trees, breathe a little fresh air, and escape the grind of the New York City advertising world I inhabited before, during, and after business hours. Those blissful days, away from my main occupation, should have told me I was longing for a different lifestyle with a greater measure of freedom.

Following your bliss will lead to unexpected opportunities

As fate would have it, Tanisha's father, John, had been an agency madman like me in his earlier life. We had a lot in common and talked frequently about the business on my visits. During one particular weekend, John asked me if I could build a website for his company. "Of course," I told him, and we began discussing his goals.

John had left the ad game in NYC in search of fresh air and relief from the grind, just as I had been seeking in micro doses. Now a real estate broker, John and his business partner, Jim, owned a firm in the area specializing in new homes in a development called Woodridge Lake. John wanted to show me around the area so I could get a feel for the community before presenting it on the website. I thought that was a great idea.

The next day, John and Jim took me on my very first tour of Woodridge Lake. It was love at first sight. I was blown away by this beautiful lakeside development. Unlike the rest of the largely rural area, the homes were modern and chic. It was an affluent community. John and Jim beamed with pride as they showed me the multiple sandy beaches, the marina, the newly built clubhouse with the Olympic size swimming pool and gym, and the eight, yes count them, eight tennis courts. The place was amazing.

Halfway between the marina and those incredible tennis courts, I casually asked John how much the vacant lots were going for. I suppose I needed to know that information in order to build the right kind of website, right? When I heard the price, I was shocked. My familiarity with the heady New York City real estate market made the ticket price seem ridiculously low.

Famous last words

Obviously, I should take the next step then and buy a vacant lot! If not me, then who? Isn't that what you do when you've dabbled in real estate and made a small killing? And after all, wasn't I the "real estate genius" who had made a killing my very first time out in New York City, the toughest of all markets? Wasn't I the guy who had quadrupled my money in only two years? Yes, I was that guy. And I got way out over my skis.

Woodridge Lake was clearly a tempting investment, but purchasing a second home was out of my price range. Buying the land without a house on it seemed like a good solution. It allowed me a gateway into this obviously high-ticket development but for a lower price. I imagined how I could sell the land for a profit inside of a year. Or better yet, I could grow into this provincial paradise and build a custom retreat from my super exciting but super stressful life in Manhattan. I could become a Connecticut landowner. I might even wear tweed. Maybe own a horse or two.

As it happened, John had a lot listed that was a little less than an acre. There were wetlands in part of the front of the lot, but the property came with plans for a home that was already approved by the environmental control board and the property owner's association—two big giant steps forward, and two big problems that I would not have to worry about. Here's the original site plan:

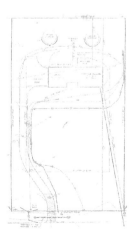

Now, here's where that second website comes in. I had recently completed creating a website for a former colleague, so I had a little chunk of money in my bank account. This, I learned, can be a dangerous thing. I wanted to invest it in something, but what? I was already putting a nice portion of my paycheck into a 401(k) from my job. I was looking to invest in something other than that kind of traditional offering.

The piece of land in Litchfield seemed like the perfect opportunity. But there was a voice in my head that kept saying, "Matt's Folly." I wondered if I was thinking clearly or if this would go down in the history of my life as a colossal failure.

It was a quiet but persistent voice. It stayed in the background until the day I sold the property, several years later. I acknowledged that voice of doubt, but eventually chose to ignore it. It was a warning sign for me to proceed with caution, which turned out to be a good thing.

Build a network of experts

As entrepreneurs, both of my parents taught me, by example, that you can take calculated risks in life and in business as long as you don't go overboard and as long as you put up safety nets up in advance so you don't free fall. My parents also taught me that if you don't know how to do something, you can figure it out. Whatever it is, sit down, apply yourself, don't be afraid to ask for help, and do what it takes to learn what you need to learn in order to achieve your goal. That turned out to be one of the most important lessons I've ever learned when it comes to just about everything.

One day when I was around seven years old my dad brought me to a property where he was working on a swimming pool. I remember how the disgusting green pool became a sparkling blue over the course of just a few days. My dad told me we owned this house. I was confused by that.

"Why do we need a second house?" I asked my dad, bewildered. After all, we already had a house that we lived in. Why did we need another one? My seven-year-old world view didn't have room for a second home. Why would we need that? My dad explained that another family would live in this second house and pay us money to live in it. A lightbulb lit up in my head. A whole new part of the world I hadn't thought about before opened up. From that day forward, I understood what it meant to own a rental property. It meant turning an algae green pool into a crystal blue oasis that others could enjoy for a reasonable price.

My mother was also an entrepreneur. She stayed at home when my sister and I were babies, but once we were in school, she went back to work. She started part time, then within a year or two moved to full time and seemed to really enjoy her profession. She was doing bookkeeping and office management at architectural firms. Then she started her own roofing company with a colleague who was an architect, and they had a nice business going for many years.

I didn't have to look much further than my folks for experts I could trust to give me good advice on this real estate investment. They had planned a trip to New York for a visit. I took them up to Litchfield and showed them the property. After the visit, my dad said the community looked beautiful but said I should ask John for "comps."

I said okay and asked John for the **comps**, though I had no idea what I was asking for. John sent over a list of comparable properties in the neighborhood and their prices. (Aha! That's what comps are.) The list showed the details of each property and the price they sold for. Comps! What a great concept! How did I not know about these?

Backstage Glossary

Comps: A price listing of comparable properties in the area, used to determine a reasonable price for a property.

My dad told me that everything seemed in line to him. He said he didn't think I would make a lot of money on this investment, but if I really liked the area, it wasn't a crazy idea. I couldn't afford to build a house yet, but with access to the lake, clubhouse, and all the other amenities, I could at least enjoy my investment in the meantime. So, although I was still haunted by the scale of my own imagination, my dad had given me the green light and helped me set up some realistic expectations. I took the plunge. In the end, my dad's crystal ball turned out to have been uncannily accurate.

Listen before you leap

That voice in the back of your head telling you to be careful is there for a reason. That inner critic is a built-in defense system designed to alert you to danger. It's there to put a doublecheck on your impulsive decisions and remind you to ask the right questions. Is this really something you can do? Will you be able to afford this? Will the numbers come out the way you planned? What is your back-up plan?

You need an advance warning system like this when you're an investor. Caution and care are important. As I write this book, I'm currently in the due diligence phase of a large apartment complex purchase. I double and triple check the numbers, looking at the deal from every possible angle to make sure I'm not missing anything.

But how do you decide to pull the trigger? How do you know whether to ignore that voice of doubt in your head or heed the warning? Is this a legitimate concern or "analysis paralysis" (when you over-analyze a deal to the point where you're unable to move forward due to fear of making an error)? How do you tell the difference? In my case, I asked my parents what they thought. But I didn't stop there. I kept expanding my circle of experts until I had enough knowledge on my team to make the boat float.

While I ultimately pushed passed the voice whispering "Matt's Folly" inside my head, I did listen enough to reach out for advice. I let the experts in my life advise me, guide me, and draw some guard rails around my expectations. By the time I took the plunge, I was pretty sure I wasn't getting in over my head—at least not financially.

Build a community of trust

It should go without saying—but unfortunately it doesn't always—that when you're trying to do something difficult, something you've never done before, it's a good idea to surround yourself with people you can trust who will tell you the truth when you need to hear it and can teach or offer you what you don't know or have. I had a lucky break in that John was my broker on the deal. I had known John for over 10 years, I was a close friend of his daughter Tanisha, and I knew he had my best interests at heart. Under normal circumstances, a broker might be looking out for their own best interests before yours. John was essentially family to me. He was someone I knew I could trust not to lead me astray. I could also count on him to hook me up with the people I would need in the community to help me get this done efficiently and economically—people I could trust.

KEYSTONE CONCEPT #6

Teamwork Makes the Dream Work

Build a community of trust and hang on to it like gold. These trusted and knowledgeable advisors are the edge that you will need to help influence big decisions, push through times of uncertainty, and lend you their expertise when you need it.

John put me in touch with a local lender who was able to arrange for financing on the property. Getting a loan on raw land can be difficult. Often, land must be purchased outright, but these lots were in a subdivision. They all had utility and sewer lines that could be connected at the street, so a local lender had no issues offering me a mortgage on my piece of property.

I put down 25% on the land, took a mortgage for the remainder, and was then the proud owner of almost an acre of tree-filled land in the middle of nowhere Connecticut, with some slight frontage drainage issues.

Here's the land when I bought it. Irresistible, right?

Woodridge Lake, Vacant Lot. 2005

And with ownership came privileges. As an owner of a property at Woodridge Lake, I had access to all the amenities—the clubhouse, the pool, all of those magnificent tennis courts and the lake itself. I bought a *cheap* used boat (that stalled countless times in the middle of the lake, requiring us to be towed back to the docks) and parked it at the marina.

When I'd visit for a weekend in the country with Len and Tanisha, we could stay at her parent's house and go to Woodridge Lake any time for some boating, swimming, fishing, or tennis. I also ventured up for day trips with friends, and we'd spend all our time at the lake. Before heading back to the city, I would drive by my tree-filled plot of land and show it to my friends and they would all be impressed with my foresight and my faith in myself and my future prospects. I myself wasn't quite as sure. I wasn't in a position to purchase a house yet, but I was able to enjoy the land a bit, get to know the area, and get a feel for living a life that stretched between two homes.

Here I am as a Connecticut landowner and skipper of my own boat, a purchase I, obviously, did not consult the experts on.

Captain Matt aboard the Melody Maker at Woodridge Lake. 2007

After a couple of years of owning the land, I thought it might be nice to spend some extended time in my part-time neighborhood. I wanted to feel more of a connection with the area and see what life would be like if I actually lived there part-time. That summer, I looked into renting a house in Woodridge for a couple of weeks. I was surprised at how much people were charging for a short-term rental. This got me to thinking—and I'm sure you know exactly what I was thinking about. I was seeing dollar signs.

A short time later, I was having lunch with a co-worker who asked me why I hadn't built anything on my property yet. I explained that cost was an issue and he asked me if I'd looked into modular homes. I hadn't thought of that but I liked the sound of being able to avoid building a house from scratch. I did some research on my own, toured a modular home factory, and discovered that there wasn't that big of a difference in terms of cost, but the quality and customization levels were widely divergent.

Down the line I learned that no matter the cost or the customization, there was absolutely no way that the Woodridge Lake Property Owner's Association was going to let me park a mobile home on my property, even if I called it "modular." In a community that could boast eight tennis courts, an Olympic-sized swimming pool and a gym, modular homes didn't really fit with the image. I should have realized this and not wasted my time, but as it turned out, I learned a lot in the process once again, by seriously investigating my options, even ones I chose not to exercise.

I now had a good idea of what the cost of building on the property would be. It wasn't as remote an option as I had thought. While it would be a stretch, it was achievable. We were toward the end of the Great Recession. I figured I would be able to get materials and labor at a discount. Maybe now was the perfect time to finally build a house on my property.

Investing is about more than money

I've since learned that no time is the perfect time, from a purely financial perspective, to build a home from scratch. First of all, it's an insane amount of work. And second, there are always overages and it always takes longer than you expect. Nonetheless, I am so glad that I went through the process because it taught me, literally from the foundation up, about what real estate is truly made of. It was a huge learning curve, and it has informed every real estate investment I've made since then. I've always believed that it helps to know the nuts and bolts of your business.

The inspiration to build a home at Woodridge Lake had always been about more than money for me. I thought initially that I would live in the home and one day take my own family there. I was coming from a place of love and creativity, inspiration and aspiration. I was making decisions the same way I did when I moved to New York to be an actor or when I started my own boutique agency. I was listening to my heart and following my nose.

I told John about my plans to begin construction and he didn't look nervous, which was reassuring. In fact, he pitched in to help. He introduced me to several local builders. After interviewing a few of them, I decided to go with Alan. I felt confident in my hire since I knew whichever builder I chose would be good, because John had introduced me. I was beginning to build a community of trust through my council of experts.

Alan listened and was patient with me, sort of like a wiser older brother. This was perfect, as I'd wandered into what was uncharted territory for me and wanted to learn as much as I could about where I was headed. I could learn from Alan, and I also felt comfortable enough to participate as fully as I wanted without worrying about stepping on his toes.

Alan had been building houses in Connecticut his entire career. We took a look at five of his properties, all in various stages of completion. The work was great. I ran my decision by John, who said he knew I was going to choose Alan and reassured me that I was making a good decision. Having John on board was critical to success in this process.

The best laid plans are flexible

Alan and I began to plan the house. Because customization was such an important element for me, I used a software program and sketched out my own ideas to share with him. I recommend doing an exercise like this, because it puts you in close communication with your builder from the beginning. It gives you a common language to express your desires and lets the builder respond and communicate the relevant issues about your vision. Here is my preliminary plan. As you can see, it's not super sophisticated, but it got the point across.

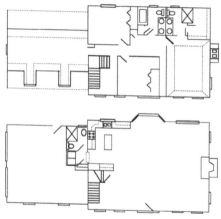

I showed my preliminary plans to Alan, who pointed out the things I needed to consider, like plumbing, electric, and air conditioning duct work. I wanted to have a large open floor plan but Alan explained that I would need a steel beam across the whole second floor if I wanted that large open space below. He also let me know how much that beam would increase the cost of construction. When I heard the number, my brilliant open floor idea went out the second-floor window.

Over the next couple of months, Alan and I went back and forth like this, making adjustments that met both of our needs while staying within the budget, or at least as close as possible. I showed the plan to friends and family and considered their input. I showed it to John to get his take, since I didn't want to do anything that would degrade the home's resale value. Once again, I tapped into my council of experts to gain as much information as I could before breaking ground.

Alan and I met in person often and produced a multitude of designs. Eventually I finalized the design and Alan priced out the work and everything was aligned and ready to go. Alan brought the design to an architect friend for a final review and an official stamp of approval. We were set!

Here is our final plan. You can see how much detail evolved through the development process.

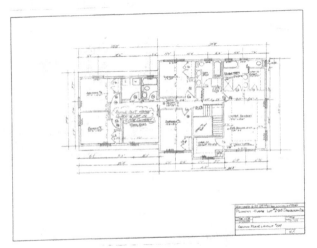

A budget called hope, with a backup plan

Next, I had to determine what all those numbers would actually mean once the rubber hit the road. The mortgage payments for the new house were going to be a stretch for me financially. I knew I could make the payments, but this was definitely going to curtail my extracurricular activities. Still, I was young and it was early in my career and I was hopeful about the future. I figured that during the next couple of years I would likely get a raise or two and that would make my payments more comfortable.

While I knew I could make it work financially if I had to, I also knew from my research on rental homes in that area that renting my house could be an option. I had a rudimentary understanding of the summer rental market at the lake. I knew how to build websites, so I could market the property with little expense. Plus I had John, who was a Realtor, to discuss this with. Although he focused on sales, he handled rentals from time to time and had a good understanding of the rates. Renting the house for a month or so during the summer would significantly reduce my out-of-pocket costs, and it wouldn't kill me to give up the house for a month or two. I could enjoy it for the rest of the year, and rent it out when the market was hot during the summer. I decided that renting the place could be a great option, just like my dad had taught me when I was a kid.

To accommodate rentals, I made some minor revisions on the plan. I created a large walk-in closet in the master bedroom with a discrete lock and key. This would be an "owner's closet," a place I could securely store my personal items within the house if I ever wanted to rent it. The master bedroom also had a smaller closet, which was certainly large enough for shorter-term tenants.

Next, I went to a local bank in Litchfield to get a **construction loan.** The builder, Alan, knew the bank president and put in a good word for me. Another score for my council of experts and a great addition to my community of trust. As collateral, I needed to provide the land, which meant I had to pay off the current mortgage. I refinanced my apartment in Manhattan and walked away from that closing with a lower rate on my co-op mortgage plus enough cash to pay off the land mortgage. Then the local bank gave me a construction loan. I paid interest only on a monthly basis until the construction was complete, at which time the loan automatically converted to a traditional 30-year mortgage.

Backstage Glossary

Construction Loan: Loans that are given in increments. As soon as different portions of the construction are complete, there is an inspection, lien waivers are provided, and then you get a "draw" from the loan to cover that portion of the work.

Next, we went ahead with applications, permits, and approvals. This part of an often-bumpy process was extremely smooth thanks to Alan. He basically presented me with some forms to sign, I wrote a few checks, and that was it. Alan had built so many other properties in the area that he knew what he was doing, he knew everybody involved, and everyone knew him. In short order, all of our permits were approved and it was time to break ground.

Bringing investment down to earth

It was a dramatic moment when I drove up to the property once construction had begun. The land was cleared and the crew was beginning to dig. All the months of planning and research; touring a modular home factory; interviewing builders and seeing their work; back and forth with Alan on the plans; the banks, mortgages and refinances; looking at other alternatives; more planning, hoping, budgeting, and permitting was now coming to fruition. At its beginning, construction pretty much looked like a hot mess.

Breaking Ground at Woodridge Lake. 2009

Every week or two I would travel to see the house progress. I watched as several cement trucks lined up along the street to pour the foundation walls.

Yep, that's me on that beam looking like I know what I'm doing, although I most certainly did not. Still, I wanted to get my hands dirty, to understand the ins and outs of construction. I wanted to bring my investment down to Earth and learn about it—all of it, as much as I possibly could under the circumstances.

Woodridge Lake House Foundation being poured. 2009

I was there when we drilled for a well to provide water to the house. I watched the progress as the house was framed out and the roof and exterior walls were installed. Electric, plumbing, HVAC, insulation, drywall, painting. Through all these steps, I gained countless insights into what it takes to build a home and all of the things that could go wrong.

I drove up to Connecticut every weekend for several months to learn about and see first-hand all the different things I had to choose: carpet and tile patterns, paint colors, fireplaces, cabinets, hardwood floor colors, countertops, appliances, fixture choices. It was overwhelming. The exercise gave me a real appreciation for all of these items I had taken for granted. Don't houses just come with those sorts of things? No, they don't. Someone has to pick them out, hinge by hinge, and that someone in this case was me.

Give a little to get a lot

The house was at last complete, at which point the loan switched over to a fully amortizing 30-year loan. I would be responsible for not only the **interest** but also the principal payments. This was the moment I had been building toward, but also a moment of truth. Was I going to rent the house? And if I didn't, could I ever take my girlfriend out to dinner again?

Backstage Glossary

Interest: Money paid to someone in return for allowing you to borrow money from them. This is paid over and above the amount borrowed to compensate the lender. This is usually determined as a certain percentage of the loan amount. That percentage is called the interest rate.

One day, out of the blue, I got a phone call from John. "Would you be open to renting your house this summer?" he said. "Someone wants if for the entire summer and they want it furnished and air conditioned." This news was good and bad. First of all, I had just completed construction and received the **C.O.**, so the house had nothing in it but carpet and paint.

Second, I had opted not to install air conditioning yet. The house had duct work and vents for it, but I hadn't bought the AC unit due to budget constraints. I was going to have to revisit that decision.

Backstage Glossary

C.O.: The Certificate of Occupancy, which is provided by the local authorities to say that a dwelling is built to code and suitable for occupancy. A building inspector will inspect the house (they usually check in at various stages of the construction) and then issue the certificate when work is complete. Without a C.O., no one is legally allowed to stay in the house.

In order to rent the property, I would have more expenses to furnish the entire house and get the AC installed. Plus, I wouldn't get to use the house for my first summer. I thought about it and ultimately decided to rent it. I could put in the AC and furnish the entire place on my credit card since I was out of cash. The rental income from that summer would cover all of those costs and by the end of it, I could start enjoying my house, only now it would be furnished and ready to go without any out-of-pocket costs.

I made sure the rental agreement we signed included a large deposit before I started incurring these costs. Then over the next couple of months, I spent every weekend at the house getting everything ordered, delivered, installed, and ready. By the time June 1 came around, the house was ready for my first tenants.

During the summer that I wasn't spending in my brand-new country house, I built a website for the property. (Yes, that would be a third website for those of you keeping score.) I chronicled the construction process with photos to invite visitors into the story of the house. Besides photos and rental prices, I also included a page that had a list of things to do in the area. I created a destination for potential tenants, to give them a feel for the whole Litchfield/Woodridge Lake experience.

Large vacation rental sites were just starting to gain traction but were virtually unknown in this marketplace, so my own website was crucial. I also listed the property on a few other vacation rental sites and, over time, these would start to bring in more guests.

As summer was coming to an end and I was getting ready to finally enjoy my new house over a glorious New England fall, I received an email though my website from a New York City couple with two young children. They wanted to rent the house for the entire winter. *What?*

It never occurred to me that anyone would want to rent my lake house in New England for the winter. Why would they want a house in a lake community off-season? It gets very cold in the winter in New England. Well, I found out that minutes from the house is a small ski mountain. It's tiny with a few short trails. Most people wouldn't plan to go there for a ski vacation, but if you have young children who are just learning to ski—it's perfect and much closer to New York City than most other ski destinations.

I happily rented the house to this family from the city. While the winter pricing was half that of the summer, it was still welcome. After crunching the numbers, it was clear to me that if I rented the house all summer and winter, with occasional renters during the fall and spring, it would cover the cost of the house for the year. I wouldn't get to enjoy my house, but it could hopefully become self-sufficient and pay for itself if it ever needed to.

Be remote but user-friendly

In time, I began to explore ways to make my rental property a little easier to manage from two hours away. Here are a few important things that I did:

Quick Tips for Remote Rentals

1. **Info:** I created a page of information about the house, laminated it, and left it at the house along with keys.

2. **Easy Access:** I had the garage door and the entrance to the house from the garage equipped with digital keypads. With this system I was able to allow new renters access to the house without the need for keys. Once a rental was confirmed, I could remotely program a code for them to access the house for specific dates.

3. **Welcoming:** Once renters entered the house for the first time, they would find a couple of sets of keys (and fobs for entrance to the marina and clubhouse) and the laminated page with info waiting for them.

4. **Local Assistance:** I hired a local cleaning team. John had a trusted person who cleaned his house. I hired her to clean the house and change the bed linens between guests. She was a nice older woman and we became friendly. She kept an eye on the house and would let me know if renters had damaged anything so I could make repairs using their security deposit.

5. **Network:** I leveraged John's contacts for other service providers in the area that I needed, such as trash hauling, lawn mowing, and snow plowing. All of these businesses were people that John knew and used himself.

I essentially became my own property manager. It was an incredible amount of work: leasing the house, coordinating move-ins and move-outs, figuring out how to get repairs done remotely. I learned a lot from managing all of these activities. The most important thing I learned was that I *did not* want to manage a short-term rental property ever again!

After that first winter, people started reaching out about rentals for the following summer. Someone approached me with a fabulous offer but they wanted the house for the entire summer. So here I was with this great house I had built to my custom specifications, but I couldn't enjoy it, and it was taking a lot of time to rent and manage the property to boot. In addition, I had been dating someone for several months, and it was quickly developing into a longer-term relationship (my now-wife Erica).

I called Erica and told her about the rental offer. Without hesitation she said, "Take it." I explained to her that I had intended to rent the house for just part of the summer and that I was hoping we would enjoy some time at the house together, "You haven't seen it yet," I said. "You haven't seen my parents' place," she responded. It turned out that her parents had a spectacular place on the other side of the state, and since they traveled a lot, we could have the place to ourselves quite often.

I took the rental for that summer. I had a few weekend rentals scheduled for the fall and another seasonal rental for that winter. There were rentals for a couple of weekends in the spring. And the entire next summer it was rented. It was starting to look like this was more of a rental property than the country home I had imagined, but I found that I was very much enjoying the opportunities this house was providing in ways that I hadn't anticipated. I found that I loved being a real estate investor. I had discovered a new passion.

Bean counting 101

With the new house, I had to tackle everybody's favorite subjects—accounting and taxes. After I purchased the land, I realized that Turbo Tax was no longer going to cut it for me. My sister referred me to someone in an accounting firm in New York that was in a networking group with her. Things were simple with the accountant when it was just the land, but once we began the construction and started renting out the property, this became a massive learning experience for me. It was during this time that I started using Excel to track expenses and eventually moved to professional accounting software.

I learned about **depreciation** and that different types of personal property depreciate on different schedules. Most importantly, I found out that there were more tax advantages if the property was not being used personally and was available for rental all year long. I could use the house for a weekend here or there—it just needed to be less than 14 nights per year. As it turned out, that's exactly what was happening.

Backstage Glossary

Depreciation: the reduction in the value of a property due to wear and tear on the asset over time.

I would stay at my house for a weekend or two during the spring and another weekend or two during the fall, and that was it. During those weekend trips, I performed maintenance on the property. So, since it truly was a full-time rental property, I was able to treat it that way and realize the tax benefits.

Know when it's time to exit

I learned a lot from the construction of that first house and management of the property and I had some transformative adventures. But as my real estate experience grew deeper, it was clear that from a numbers perspective, it wasn't the best investment in history. While I was able to get close to breaking even on a yearly basis, I was not cash-flow positive. I did a lot of work managing the property and the short-term tenants, but I wasn't getting anything in return for all that work. I was learning the final lesson from the house: knowing when it is time to sell.

I just about broke even on the sale but the experience was more than I could ever have imagined on every level, and it taught me more than I realized along the way. From the construction of a house, to marketing and dealing with tenants, to learning accounting matters, the experience of building this house from the ground up was an unbelievably amazing process. I didn't know it at the time, but it is what set me on the path to become a full-time real estate investor.

Completed Woodridge Lake House. 2010

CHAPTER 4 LESSONS LEARNED

- Build a community of trust with trusted advisors and experts to avoid costly mistakes and missed opportunities.

- Pay expert third parties for their review. It will be worth it.

- Know when to ignore that voice of doubt and when to listen closely.

- Market comps are extremely informative and important when considering a purchase or a sale.

- Understanding loans for construction—permanent and refinancing—is helpful, but remember to engage your community of trust in these transactions.

- Learn what a house is made of from the ground up: A working knowledge of the systems in the house, electric, water, gas, sewer, HVAC is helpful when something breaks and needs to be replaced.

- Learn about how to manage your business finances and what tax codes apply to you.

- Automate wherever possible to recapture your time for more productive activities.

- Managing properties is a difficult business.

- Marketing your property can go a long way and minimize your vacancy.

- Most importantly, make sure the property cash flows! Otherwise, you are speculating instead of investing.

THE ACCIDENTAL HOUSE HACK

B efore I rush you headlong into my next fly-by-the-seat-of-my-pants property investment, I want to reassure you that you are in good hands. I had a "real" job for many, many years and that taught me a lot about how to make sound, creative business and investment decisions. Here's how my professional history prepared me for my experiences in real estate.

My life as an advertising tycoon

After my fleeting life on the stage and my accidental foray into the world-wide web, I began climbing the treacherous ladder of the advertising industry. This is a world so notoriously demanding, so all-consuming and competitive, that it is captured in shows like *Mad Men* for a very good reason.

After 18 years of competing in that three-ring circus, I became a seasoned digital marketing executive with a proven track record of effective digital media development. I was central in the ideation, creation, and management of complex web development projects and online marketing campaigns for Fortune 500 companies like Pfizer, Sony, Maxell, Arista Records, IBM, Coca-Cola, Morgan Stanley, and the U.S. Department of Energy. Yes, even *the* United States Department of Energy, as it turns out, needs an advertising campaign from time to time.

I'm also a PMI Certified Project Management Professional (PMP) with a proven ability to manage and direct personnel to plan, implement, and complete cutting-edge projects in high-pressure, rapidly changing environments—I'm a marketing veteran whose New York City career spanned several of the world's largest advertising agencies, producing award-winning projects. I ran the gamut during my 18 years in the ad biz, and it was worth every second, but it wasn't easy. Now, I have the benefit of extensive business experience to put to good work in my real estate career.

So on to Brooklyn and my first important lesson about the value of personal space. Unless you are a mushroom, you need light and space in which to grow. And in New York, space equals big bucks, and big bucks mean working even harder when you are already working as hard as you can. Or it means finding a better deal outside of Manhattan. And since I wanted to spend more time with the love of my life, not less, I chose the latter. But let me back up for a second and fill you in on my very own sweeping and spectacular New York love story.

When Matt Met Erica

Right around the time that I was completing the house in Connecticut, I met a smart and beautiful woman named Erica. We met on a new online dating platform that I was beta testing at the time. One day I logged in and—lo and behold!—there was Erica, the love of my life, although I didn't know that yet. As it turns out, we had both suggested the same potential date, a walk on New York's Highline, a newly opened, beautiful elevated park built along the tracks of an abandoned supply train.

We met, we walked, we talked and found out that we had so many things in common, including a love for the theater. I remember Erica talking so passionately about art—theater in particular—and about its ability to make a social impact and create societal change. Her passion for the arts and their educational and transformative powers was impressive. She wasn't someone who liked the theater simply because it was fun. She worked on the business side of the industry, and she wasn't there just to meet celebrities. She was there for the ultimate impact that she felt she could make on the world, and she saw the theater as a positive force for good.

Erica blew me away. We were a perfect fit from the start. After that first walk on the Highline, we dated for about a year and a half, and then I took her back to the Highline and proposed. Thank God, Erica said, "Yes." Look what a lucky man I am.

Matt & Erica on the Highline. 2012.

Erica and I were married on a beautiful Labor Day weekend in Connecticut. The ceremony and reception were held at The Eugene O'Neill Theater Center, where new playwrights of the American stage are born, people like

August Wilson, John Guare, and yes, even *Hamilton*'s iconic playwright, Lin-Manuel Miranda.

The O'Neill is a stunning and romantic spot nestled into the Connecticut coastline, and it was and is an important part of our lives. We wholeheart-edly support the work they do in bringing spectacular new voices of the stage to life. We had the ceremony in The Edith Oliver Theater, an outdoor performance space. And then a reception in the sunken garden that over-looks an amazing field with the ocean in the distant background.

Erica & Matt's Wedding. 2012. Photos by Courtney Lindberg

Growth requires adequate space

It was a glorious time in my life, and I began planning for a future with my new family. This, of course, meant that we needed more space. Fortunately, my future looked bright and my income was on the rise, which is important when you're contemplating more square footage. I had been working at R/GA where I was brought in to lead the project management team on the Verizon Telecom account. FiOS was the big initiative back then, and we were in charge of the strategy, design, and development of their website and online advertising campaign. This was a massive piece of business for the agency and I was directly responsible for the financials on the $30 million dollar account.

When I came onboard, the agency had won the account about 90 days prior, and it was a huge mess. I singlehandedly built a financial reporting structure to be able to meet with the clients to show them their budget burn rate against their retainer past, present and future. This garnered me huge accolades both with the client and internally, leading to a nice promotion. As if all of that work wasn't enough, I worked on a few special projects including development of R/GA's global intranet and 2011 Cannes presentation.

While I enjoyed the work for nearly 3 years at R/GA, I was offered an incredible opportunity to join an agency called MRY that specialized in social media and youth marketing. I believed this was the future of advertising, and I wanted to get experience and bring myself up to speed working with this group. I came onboard as a group program director at MRY, which was led by the brilliant and innovative Matt Britton. I had portfolio oversight of top-tier clients including Visa, Gillette, and Coca-Cola.

While I was at MRY, Erica and I decided to expand our family. Very shortly afterward, Erica was pregnant and it was time to contemplate a move. This was when Brooklyn came into the picture. We loved our one-bedroom apartment on the Upper West Side of Manhattan but we knew things would get a bit cramped with the new addition to our family. We started to look for a two-bedroom place in our neighborhood. Again, I love the Upper West Side. Again, it was sooooo expensive.

It was beginning to look like expanding our square footage was going to take a real bite out of our budget, so Erica suggested that we drive around Brooklyn and take a look. We had no intention of moving to Brooklyn, but so many of our friends had said it would be perfect for us, we figured we would take a look so we could tell people we'd explored it and it wasn't for us.

I had lived in New York for over 22 years at this point but had only been to Brooklyn a handful of times. People commute from the boroughs into Manhattan, rarely vice versa. When you live in Manhattan, the boroughs might as well be a million miles away. Hence, I didn't really know the area at all, but I did know that a lot of people moved there when they were ready to have a family and needed more space.

Erica and I spent a weekend driving around the different neighborhoods, and much to our surprise, we really liked Brooklyn. It reminded me of the New York City I had moved to and loved in the early 1990s. We explored a bit further and discovered that both of our commutes to work would be exactly the same length as they were from the Upper West Side if we found a place near one of the first few subway stops into Brooklyn.

We zoomed in on a couple of neighborhoods that met all the criteria and started going to open houses. We realized that our friends had been right: we really could get a lot more for our money in Brooklyn. Instead of a small two-bedroom in Manhattan, we were looking at three-bedroom apartments for the same price, and some even had outdoor space!

After some serious hunting, we found a place that we liked. In addition to the main three-bedroom apartment, it also had a separate one-bedroom rental unit upstairs. I started thinking about that. Sure, the place would cost a little more, but the rental income would more than make up for that. And after managing a property two hours away in Connecticut, I knew I could handle a rental in the same building. This opened up some new horizons. Maybe I was searching for an even larger property than I thought.

I reached out to the owners of the property to schedule a tour with Erica but they told me they had already accepted an offer. I was disappointed but not surprised. At least I knew I was looking for the right things. That property had been right on the money, and even though it was Brooklyn, the place sold in a Manhattan minute. But I was on to a different kind of deal now and while I didn't realize it, I was on the path to my very first **house hack**.

Backstage Glossary

House Hack: Purchase a two- to four-unit property and live in one unit while renting the other unit(s) to cover or reduce the mortgage payments. After at least one year, you can move out and rent your old unit as well, covering all your expenses (mortgage included) and resulting in a profit— positive cash flow.

Think big, but understand your boundaries

I came across a 5-unit property that was run down and needed a ton of work. The floor plans were a mess, we would need to knock down walls and move kitchens, and the basement needed to be built-out as well. A large amount of work was needed, but there was a ton of potential. Erica did not share my optimism. She was not keen on the idea of DIY renovation going on with a newborn in the house, especially a renovation of this scale. Erica is a sensible person, and this is one of the many reasons I married her. So, I listened to my wife and we said no to the fixer upper with our baby on the way.

But now I thought, if two rental units were good, why wouldn't five rental units be even better? Imagine the palace we could buy with that kind of a rent roll. Fortunately for me, my friend Jon, who was acting as our real estate agent, gently explained that the financing on buildings that are five or more units are structured completely differently. Thankfully, he steered me clear of all that on the front end and told me to limit myself to no more than four units.

Keep your options open until the deal is sealed

I now knew that two to four units would be the sweet spot. We continued looking and then we found a great single unit in a larger building. It had an elevator that opened into the unit – it was a floor-through, occupying the entire floor and sprawling with three bedrooms and two balconies. The place was just breathlessly Brooklyn chic. We put in an offer, but then a new listing popped up just around the corner that caught my eye, a two-unit townhome. We went and checked it out just in case.

It turned out that this second property was even better! The owner's unit was downstairs and it had a backyard, which is rare and desirable in this urban area. It was a legal two-bedroom apartment, but had a third room that was a perfect nursery. The upstairs unit was a three-bedroom, 2.5 bath unit that had tenants in place who had been there a few years. The place was a dream deal.

There was one problem, which in my view, was actually an opportunity. The property was located next door to an abandoned KFC that was a genuine eyesore. It was horrifying enough to have scared away any buyers, so the price was reasonable. Where others saw the decaying corpse of a failed fast-food restaurant, I saw a vacant lot in an up-and-coming area.

We determined that, eventually, someone would purchase that property and build some nice condos. If we were right, this could lift our property value and maybe we could sell the extra development rights, aka **air rights**, that our property was already zoned for.

> **Backstage Glossary**
>
> **Air Rights:** Development rights that can be transferred to a neighboring property. These grant the owner the right to build additional square footage on their property. When someone sells air rights, they still keep their own property.

The location was great. It was a few blocks from the newly developed Barclays Center, which had virtually every subway line running to it. Looking in the opposite direction, we weren't too far from the first (and only, at the time) Whole Foods in Brooklyn. And it was a really nice Whole Foods. While the block the property was on wasn't the greatest, it was in the immediate path of progress. We knew we'd be next.

This strategic approach had done wonders for me in Washington Heights. The property on the Upper West Side—the one that required a new floor when I moved in—didn't do quite as well because that area was already developed, though I was happy with the value increase. But properties in areas that are on their way up have larger increases. So, we made an offer on the property and it was accepted!

KEYSTONE CONCEPT #7
Follow the Path of Progress

Look for positive signs of social and economic growth. New employers, restaurants, transportation, and housing development are all good indicators that an area is on an upswing and has a good chance to be a wise investment in the future.

Avoid red tape by thinking creatively

Moving to Brooklyn meant a life change for us, and for me in particular. I would no longer own a property in Manhattan, which was kind of a psychological shift for me since I'd become a die-hard Manhattanite. It was time to learn the incredible power of letting go of my beloved Upper West Side.

My place on the UWS was a co-op and while I wanted to hold on to it, there was just too much red tape to cope with. The co-op rules at the time allowed for rentals but they needed to be approved by the board and the rules could be changed at any time. The rental income would have covered the mortgage payments, but with no cash flow. Even selling that apartment might present challenges because the co-op had to approve the buyer.

I put the property on the market myself (without a broker) at a somewhat aggressive price. I had several showings and eventually found a buyer. As I mentioned, all sales needed to be approved by the co-op board, and I had to recuse myself from the discussion due to the conflict of interest. I found out the next day that the board did not approve the buyer.

Apparently, there was something a little less than traditional about her finances, but in my opinion it didn't warrant a denial. I thought that was overkill and I was upset with the board. My friend Jon suggested that I put it back on the market but add $50K to the price. I thought this was a crazy idea and told him so. He agreed but said that then I could come down $50K in negotiating with a prospective buyer, and they would feel like they were getting a great deal. I figured it was worth a shot.

I listed the unit and set the first open house for a couple of days later. I had a broker reach out to me who had a client who was very interested and wanted to see it before the open house. They came, saw the place, and within five minutes after leaving the apartment called and made me a full price offer, which I gladly accepted. This person had impeccable financials and was quickly approved by the board. Thanks to the board's original denial and my friend's crazy idea, I ended up with an extra $50,000 in my pocket. Erica and I were Brooklyn-bound with a fist full of money to renovate our new townhome.

We made a number of changes to our unit in Brooklyn before we moved in. We installed new lighting, replaced the hardwood floors, built closets, updated the kitchen, added a fresh coat of paint, and "gut renovated" the master bathroom.

Erica was impressed that I seemed to know exactly what to do, where to go, what to buy, and that I understood all the options. I was definitely scoring points because—after building the Woodridge Lake house from scratch and picking out all of those fixtures—it was easy to look like a pro on this reduced scale and impress Erica, which I love to do.

The financials on the property worked out well for us. We were able to get a 30-year mortgage at a low, fixed **interest rate**. Our upstairs tenant's rent covered a majority of the mortgage, so our portion of the monthly payments ended up being a lot lower than comparable places in the neighborhood. If we ever needed to move out, we could rent our unit for more money than the upstairs unit because of the renovations and, of course, that amazing backyard.

Backstage Glossary

Interest Rate: The percentage of a loan that is paid over and above the amount borrowed to compensate the lender. The rate can be at a "fixed" amount that doesn't change for the entire loan, or it can be a "floating" rate that changes depending on certain conditions.

And this is how, without even realizing it, I managed to pull off my very first "house hack." The next time you're apartment shopping, remember me, and think BIG.

CHAPTER 5 LESSONS LEARNED

- Taking the time to establish a solid foundation in any business venture is never a waste.

- Be willing and able to invest in your passions.

- Think big, but respect your own boundaries, as well as the rules that will regulate the cost of your dreams.

- Don't hang on to a property for sentimental reasons if it's going to wind you in red tape. Learn to let go, it's freeing, teaches you confidence, and offers a lesson in the true value of things.

- Lessons you learn the hard way pay off for a lifetime. There is no school like the school of hard knocks, and no teacher like first-hand experience.

- Never discount input from your wife. Her unique perspective can shine light on your blind spots.

CHAPTER 6

TAKING MY SHOT

Our life in Brooklyn came to an end when Erica got that job offer in Miami that she could not turn down. I thought carefully about my next step for some months after arriving back in the state of my birth and realized it was fruitless to try to rebuild an advertising career in Florida after working in the Big Apple. I could never get to scale in such a small market, and I was burned out. This is when I made the decision to embrace what had always been a passion hovering just off stage through every act of my life, and to try make real estate investment my day job.

On January 1, 2016, I started my new career as a real estate investor. I am nothing if not chronologically precise when I'm turning over a new leaf. And there's a reason for that. I'm a planner. That's turned out to be helpful.

We had settled into our life in Miami and now that I was a full-time investor, I had to schedule my time. What was I going to do with myself during working hours? I remembered that in *Rich Dad, Poor Dad* Robert Kiyosaki had mentioned that you should go to seminars. It will likely cost money, he said, but it will be worth it. Even if the seminar content is terrible, you will get to network with other like-minded individuals. I don't remember the exact words, but the gist of it was that one day a seminar would come to town, and when it did, I should sign up.

You get what you pay for

A few days later—out of nowhere—I heard an advertisement on the car radio that there was a real estate seminar coming to town. I pulled off to the side of the road and wrote down the phone number (just like my dad used to when he saw those "For Sale by Owner" signs). It had to be kismet, because it had happened just like Kiyosaki said it would.

When I got home, I made the call and, just like that, I was registered for a free seminar on real estate investing. Notice I use the word "free." The seminar was conducted at a hotel and lasted an hour or two. They told us about their program and said that they had just a few spots left at their next upcoming seminar, so if we were interested we'd better hurry! They said that if I ran to the back of the room and paid a couple of hundred bucks right now, I could be one of the lucky few to get into the seminar. Now, I wasn't born yesterday. I come from the ad world and I know an urgency play when I hear one.

But then I remembered what Kiyosaki had said, and in the big scheme of things a couple hundred bucks wasn't too steep of a price to see how this thing would play out since I was starting from scratch. So, I forked over the cash.

Long story short, I signed up for the "Real Estate Investing and **Tax Lien** Crash Course" for the next weekend. I had a shiny new bag with prep materials to prove I was a genuine and serious aspiring real estate professional. When I told Erica what I had done, I think she thought I was a little nuts, but she played along because she loves me. Besides, I had to start somewhere, and it wasn't as crazy as trying to make a living as an actor. So, I had some wiggle room. The bar wasn't all that high yet.

> ### Backstage Glossary
>
> **Tax Lien:** A lien placed on a property to ensure the payment of taxes. The laws vary from state to state but purchasing these liens from the municipalities that impose them can result in very large returns or possibly ownership of the property.

I went to the seminar and I have to say, I did meet some very interesting people. The content actually wasn't too bad. They provided a full binder with information, several CDs of audio training, and they taught their entire process in a single weekend.

At the end, they tried to upsell us into a mentorship program for thousands of dollars. I declined the mentorship but I liked their system. I thought I would give it a shot (*Hamilton* pun intended). Thus began my brief but illuminating career in tax liens and foreclosures where I learned, once again, you get what you pay for.

When in doubt, scope it out

I felt better after the weekend seminar because at least now I had a plan. I would work through these tax liens. I would find properties at a great price, fix them up, and then flip them. What could be simpler?

I planned on investing the money I generated from flipping these mega-cheap tax lien properties into buy-and-hold rental properties that would provide a small but passive stream of income. Do this for a few years, build a small empire, I'm home free. What could go wrong?

Well, let me just say one thing about my plan: there is a reason they make reality shows about this career path.

As I began exploring the area, I quickly realized that real estate in Miami was on one extreme or the other. There were pricey properties and dirt-cheap properties and almost nothing in the middle. I didn't have deep enough pockets to start flipping million-dollar homes, but neither did I want to be renovating in dangerous neighborhoods. Finding a middling sweet spot was turning out to be a real challenge in my area.

I started casting about for alternative markets, just like my full binder of seminar materials told me to do. This brought my cousin Marcus to mind. Marcus lives in a nice suburb between Cleveland and Akron, Ohio, more than 1,000 miles north of Miami. Well, they had said to look at alternate markets, and this was one where I had a decent connection.

KEYSTONE CONCEPT #8

Explore Other Markets

It's okay to invest out of state. Invest where the numbers make sense, even if it's not in your backyard.

Marcus and I have a close relationship. He was the best man at my wedding and I am the godfather of his son. I called him up, told him my plan, and asked if I could stay at their place for a week while I explored their area. He said, "Of course." I also asked if he knew a real estate agent I could speak with. He got a recommendation from a friend and connected us. As you can see, Marcus is top shelf.

I spoke with the real estate agent and explained what I was looking to do. She said she would help. "Great," I said. I went back to working the system I was taught, tracking down tax liens in the area. The process took a few weeks and during this time the agent ghosted me for no apparent reason. This abrupt ending wound up being a blessing in disguise because when the first agent dematerialized, I met Rich.

It was an interesting coincidence meeting Rich, just one of those random things you stumble on along the way and then spend the rest of your life wondering what you would have done if it hadn't have happened—how close you came to missing out on your shot.

I was talking with the county clerk in Ohio, getting some info on the liens one morning, and she asked who was doing the title work for me. I said I didn't have anyone yet and asked her if she could recommend someone. She told me she wasn't allowed to do that, but she did mention that a lot of people tend to use a guy named Tim whose family had been in the business for generations. That sounded pretty good to me.

I tracked Tim down and I told him I was interested in flipping properties. He said I had to meet his son's friend Rich who was a real estate agent in the area who had some success in the house-flipping world. I met Rich and I never looked back. Rich was and is quite a character with a fantastic sense of humor and a gregarious personality. He really knew what he was doing and did it all with a smile. He also drove the most amazing green van I've ever seen. He was exactly the guy I needed.

Rich's Amazing Green Machine.

I had found four target properties that were going to auction at the courthouse the next day. Rich and I drove by all the properties to size them up. One of the houses was completely abandoned and on a quiet road, so we walked up to the house and peered through the windows to try to get a sense of what was inside.

You aren't allowed to go inside tax lien properties in advance. Properties are listed and auctioned off sight unseen. You get what you get. No inspections allowed. This, I was to discover, is a dicey situation at best. Think *Storage Wars* but for houses!

I arrived at the courthouse for my very first auction, and by the time it started there were only two properties left on the docket out of the four that I had been interested in. The other two had been removed. I came to learn that this is common. People often come up with the money to pay their tax bill at the last minute to stop the sale. The other two properties sold at prices far above my limit. That first day, I walked away empty handed.

I also walked away very surprised at the amount of money people were paying for the properties. I couldn't make money at those prices. It would leave me no profit margin at all. The people who were bidding and winning the properties all looked like contractors, and as it turned out, that's exactly what they were. The contractors would bid on the properties and basically buy themselves a job. It's good work if you can get it, but this put me in an unenviable position on the food chain.

If a contractor bought the property, the profit was built into their own contracting work. There didn't need to be additional profit for the investor, because they were the investor. This meant they could pay more for the property than I could and still come out ahead. I couldn't afford to pay for the property and pay a contractor—who makes a profit—and still make a profit for myself. There was no way for me to compete in this market.

This is where Rich's real value to came to light. He and I had really hit it off, so he started working hard to find good flip opportunities through several channels he had access to that I did not. While he was searching in Ohio, I continued following my seminar binder a little closer to home in Florida.

Florida didn't turn out any better results. At one point I went to an auction where a central Florida condo was on the docket. Having done research prior to the auction, I knew there were two identical units (same size, same floor) in the same building that were listed for sale and had been on the market for several weeks, so there wasn't any competition for them. The auctioned property sold for a price higher than the traditionally listed properties. The absurdity blew my mind! The listed properties could be inspected and the auctioned property was being purchased sight unseen and at a higher price. This exemplifies how people can get swept up in the frenzy of an auction, or don't do their homework, or both.

After many failed attempts, I gave up on the auctions in Florida. Besides those who didn't do their research or got swept up in auction fever or were speculators, there was also a lot of foreign money from South America flowing into the market and being parked in a place with a more stable government. Properties were going for unbelievable prices. So, for many different reasons, the Florida market didn't make sense for me. It was the same math. Ultimately, I threw that binder away and decided I would stop pursuing tax lien auctions, but as it turns out, I wasn't quite done yet. I still had to live the whole house flipping thing out, and I was about to get my opportunity, thanks to my new best friend, Rich.

While I had been chasing liens in Florida, Rich had found some promising properties in Ohio and I ended up purchasing something at last. But before I had even completed the first flip, Rich and I were onto a second property, and that second property, was a doozy. Once I got into it, I found mold and bad plumbing and electrical. It was a complete mess and cost way more to renovate than I expected. While it was beautiful in the end, I went over budget on it. I had made a good profit on the first flip and lost about half of that profit on the second one. My biggest takeaway from these flips was that I will never buy another property that I am unable to inspect prior to purchase. There are just too many unknowns that can be unbelievably costly.

Podcast University

I did a lot of driving during my time in Miami. Our daughter was going to school about 20 minutes from our house. It was very close to where Erica was working, but there were many times when I drove our daughter to school or picked her up. During pickup time, the drive was often 40+ minutes due to traffic. Driving my daughter to school along with driving around town and making the four-hour trip to see my folks in Orlando, I found ways to put all that time in the car to good use. This is when I officially enrolled in what I call "Podcast University."

Instead of listening to the radio on my car rides, I started listening to real estate podcasts to find out what I didn't know. It's in my DNA to take whatever business or craft I undertake very seriously, and real estate was no exception. I listened to anything and everything, and let me tell you, there is a veritable tidal wave of real estate podcasts out there and no clear way to know ahead of time which ones are not worth your time.

My wife and I found it hilarious that our two-year-old daughter could perfectly recite the introductions to a few of my favorite podcasts. My daughter was in the car with me a lot and I told her that she was going to know more about real estate than anyone by the time she was five. Of course she doesn't remember any of that now, but I definitely laid down a foundation, just like my dad had done for me way back when he showed me that pool when I was seven.

I've heard it said that you should surround yourself with people you want to be like. I didn't really know anyone who was in the kind of real estate business I wanted to create. So, I listened to the podcasts, hunting for kindred spirits and taking in their special knowledge. Although there weren't podcasts back then, this is exactly what I'd done when I went to New York to be an actor all those years ago without even knowing who Stephen Sondheim was, or those days when I didn't know what an HTML tag was. Time for another deep dive of immersion.

While listening to these podcasts, beyond getting a rudimentary education in the basics of real estate, I was experiencing a gradual shift in my mindset. I was beginning to think like a real estate investor.

So, for those of you who don't have the thousands of hours to spend enrolled in Podcast-U that I did, here is your cheat sheet with some of the basics I picked up that helped me understand the business.

School's In Session

Welcome to the
Backstage Version of Podcast University

Five Ways that Real Estate Makes Money:

1. **Cash Flow**
   Profit that is the result of rent received minus the properties expenses. With diligent underwriting and management, this can be steady and predictable. This is my main focus with real estate investing.

2. **Appreciation**
   The amount that a property goes up in value. This can be the result of many different factors and is not easily predictable. If the real estate market does not perform well, or your location becomes undesirable, your property could even lose value. I look for opportunities where I can force this appreciation by making improvements, but in all cases, I do not count on market appreciation.

3. **Debt Pay Down**

The portion of the rental income that goes to pay down the principal balance on your loan. Your tenant is paying down your loan for you and you are gaining equity in the property.

4. **Tax Benefits**

There are many tax benefits for owning real estate, depending on your particular tax situation. The single largest benefit is depreciation, which often allows you to use most, or all, of your yearly cash-flow without paying income tax on it. Be sure to check with your CPA about this and about depreciation recapture.

5. **Inflation Hedge**

Have you ever heard someone say something like, "back in my day a carton of milk was only 10 cents?" With inflation, the value of a dollar becomes less over time. You are borrowing (usually 75% of the price of a property) from the bank using today's dollars. But you are paying them back over the next 30 years. The value of those dollars becomes less every year, but you don't have to pay more.

Commercial vs Residential

Every piece of real estate is broken down into two types—commercial or residential. Commercial real estate can be further divided into retail, industrial, and office space. Residential real estate basically comes in two forms. There's standard residential which you're probably familiar with, ranging from a single-family home to a four-unit property. Then there are the properties of five units or more, which are an entirely different category. As my friend Jon mentioned when my wife and I were looking at properties in Brooklyn, these larger properties are underwritten differently. The most significant difference between the two is the way that the financing world treats them when you're looking to get a mortgage.

Getting started

Most real estate investors start by investing in single-family properties. I invested passively in a couple of single-family properties and it's been tremendously successful. One of the ways you can do this is by utilizing a "turnkey" provider. What turnkey providers do is find great real estate deals and sell them to investors. They usually are a large operation with phenomenal real estate connections so they can acquire deals at a substantial savings. The properties they purchase are run-down. The company buys the property, renovates it, then turns around and sells it to an investor. Often they'll have a management company that manages the property for you for a small fee. They make a little bit of money on the sale of the property, but the real profit for them comes from those management fees.

If you pursue this route, do some extreme due diligence because not all providers are equal. I recommend that you purchase property from someone who has their own management company. I've heard horror stories about people who buy from one company and then have to deal with a different group for management. The two can end up pointing fingers at each other. "Well, we had to do so many repairs on the property because they didn't renovate it properly," and other nonsense. When it's all with one company, no one can pass the buck.

These turnkey properties seem great and the **cash-on-cash** return can be phenomenal. So, why did I move on from them? Well, it's because they weren't scalable when I sat down and looked at the numbers.

Backstage Glossary

Cash-on-Cash Return: The profit that is made based on the amount of cash that was invested into a deal. If you buy a $60,000 house that costs you $20,000 (down payment and closing costs) and the property gives you $2,000 of positive cash flow each year, that would be a 10% cash-on-cash return. ($2,000 / $20,000 = 10%.)

If your cash flow averages $200 per month per door and you have ten properties, that's $2,000 per month or $24,000 a year. I'd certainly be happy with an extra $24,000 per year, but the problem is that you've hit the ceiling. You're not going to be able to go any further, so if you're looking to get to a point where you have some massive passive income—where you are able to reduce your work hours or even quit your job and live off passive income—that's not going to happen. Why? Well, it comes down to the financing.

Financing

There are different kinds of financing for single-family (up to four unit) properties and it is the best type of financing you can get. It's the biggest advantage to investing in this category: you can get a 30-year, fully **amortizing** mortgage at a fixed interest rate (your interest rate is often lower if the property is going to be your primary residence—like in a house hack).

> ### Backstage Glossary
>
> **Amortization:** The amount of time over which a loan's payments are calculated. This is generally 30 years for a standard single-family home and often shorter for a commercial loan. Commercial loan terms are usually shorter than their amortization, resulting in a large balance that is due at the end of the loan.

The issue comes when you want to grow and acquire more than 10 properties. These great mortgages are available to consumers because of **Fannie Mae** and **Freddie Mac**, which are backed by the federal government. That incentivizes banks to approve mortgages by giving them some assurances. But the Fannie and Freddie guidelines, at the time of writing this book, limit you to 10 properties per person. Some banks will actually only go up to six or seven properties but there are lenders who will go to the full 10. Once you get past that magic number, the financing available to you is the same as on a commercial loan. We will get into that in more detail later, but it's not fully amortizing, 30-year fixed-rate debt, and the rates are potentially higher. So when you work through the numbers, it's not scalable to create a large amount of passive income solely through smaller sized properties.

Backstage Glossary

Fannie Mae: The Federal National Mortgage Association (FNMA) is a U.S. government-sponsored enterprise. It may be referred to as a type of "agency debt." The organization was formed in 1938 during the Great Depression by the U.S. Congress to expand the mortgage market. Essentially, the organization helps lenders provide debt at favorable interest rates by reducing the lender's risk by guaranteeing the loan.

Freddie Mac: The Federal Home Loan Mortgage Corporation (FHLMC) is a U.S. government-sponsored enterprise. It may be referred to as a type of "agency debt." The organization was formed in 1970 to compete with Fannie Mae. Essentially, the organization helps lenders provide debt at favorable interest rates by reducing the lender's risk by guaranteeing the loan.

Freedom from debt is not the same as financial freedom

The single biggest takeaway from my time in Podcast University is the understanding that being debt free is different from being financially free. I wanted to be financially free, but I'd been focusing on becoming debt free. I needed to fix that.

I'd been looking at things the way I was originally taught to look at them: in school, by my parents, and by "financial experts." They taught me that I need to be debt free in order to be financially free. But it doesn't actually work that way, and sometimes these two are mutually exclusive paths.

> # KEYSTONE CONCEPT #9
> ## You Want to Be Financially Free
> Being debt free is vastly different from being financially free. Don't be afraid to maintain debt in order to increase your investment potential. Use leverage to increase your returns, just do it responsibly.

The old maxim that told you to work hard, live within your means, and stay debt free isn't always the best path to financial freedom anymore.

At first glance, and in many instances, being debt free makes complete sense. You can bury yourself under debt from credit cards, car loans, or a mortgage you can't afford. These are examples of bad debt; they tie back into the liabilities we talked about earlier in the book. They're all examples of cash flowing out of your pocket instead of into it. You can get to the point where just paying the interest alone is overwhelming, and you still have the mountain of debt weighing you down.

I had a home mortgage and some credit cards that I usually paid off every month. I was successfully on my path to becoming debt free. That's good; credit card debt has ridiculous interest rates. But I learned that if you really want to grow your real estate holdings, paying off your mortgage won't let you go as far or as quickly as prudently leveraged property will.

To be clear, I'm not saying that people should live outside of their means. No one should pile on debt—definitely a bad idea. Leverage is a massive multiplier—it magnifies. Keep in mind this works on both ends: profits and losses. Properly amplifying debt can amplify profit, but it must be used responsibly. What's that line from *Spider-Man*? "With great power comes great responsibility." Real estate is the only investment I know of where you can borrow up to 80% from the bank and keep all the profits. However, you can also lose it all if you can't make your debt payments, so you've got to proceed with caution.

Here's an exercise to help you make the same mental leap that I did.

Leverage Exercise

For this exercise, we will assume the value of each property goes up, or appreciates, by 3% each year (which is lower than the 4% to 6% U.S. national average). Let's say you have $200K to invest in real estate.

Scenario 1: You buy a $200K property, all cash. After five years, at 3% compounding interest, the value is now $231,855. A $31,855 profit, not bad!

Scenario 2: You put 25% down on 4 properties ($50K each). You have now purchased $800K of real estate but you owe the bank $600K. After five years, at 3% compounding interest, the value is now $927,419. After you pay the bank back the $600K for the mortgage, you are left with $327,419. Which is a $127,419 profit. This doesn't include the amount of mortgage paid down over five years of monthly payments.

In this example, we can see that Scenario 2, which used debt, produced four times the profit than purchasing one property outright. Does that quadrupling of the initial investment sound familiar? This is what we talked about in Chapter 3 with the property I purchased in Washington Heights.

Keep in mind that these scenarios did not factor in the other ways that investors make money from real estate, some of which would be amplified by having four properties vs just one.

The case of my amazing friend Aaron and his 15-year mortgage

I met Aaron when I was about to move to Boston (we will get to that in a couple of chapters). I have a cousin who was living in that area and she was renting a house from Aaron. While I was looking for a place to move into, she put us in touch. Although he didn't have anything that was a good fit for my family, I liked him. I thought he was probably a good guy to know in the area and I decided to keep in touch.

I reached out to Aaron once we had completed our move. He turned out to be one of the nicest people I've ever met. Erica and I have gotten to know him and his wife well. Isn't real estate great? It's all about communities of trust and lasting friendships.

Aaron and I talk about real estate often. He works in the industry, and over many years has built up quite an impressive portfolio of rental properties (usually duplexes) in fantastic locations. Over time, he has acquired superb assets in one of the most desirable areas in the country. Each property is worth a substantial amount of money.

The two of us were talking about his portfolio one day and he told me his plan: He had recently refinanced all of his properties into one large 15-year multimillion-dollar portfolio loan. He has calculated that the rent from all the units combined will cover all operating costs and the loan.

Aaron is "wicked smart" as they say in Massachusetts. His underwriting is solid. He's owned his properties for a while, he knows what the costs are to maintain them, and he's worked in a buffer for unexpected costs. He will do great with this plan. The issue is, he needs to wait 15 years for his plan to work out. In 15 years, once everything is paid off, he can retire and live off the income generated by these houses. Then, he'll be living the dream. It's a great plan. Only…what about the next 15 years of his life?

Until Aaron retires in a decade and a half, he will be living under the shadow of this large debt with nothing to show for it. He does well in his business, but he needs to continue working for the next 15 years to pay for his primary residence, put food on the table, take care of his kids, and all the rest. If he were to have a 30-year mortgage, his payments would be lower and he would have extra cash flow. He could use that cash flow to pay for things in his life. Yes, he would have the debt for 15 years more than his current plan, but he could have a better quality of life, for more of his life.

Aaron's point of view on this is that with a 30-year mortgage, he will have to pay a lot more interest, since he has the debt for twice as long. And when I say "a lot more," it's over $1.5 million more in interest payments. That's pretty substantial. He makes enough money to be able to comfortably pay the mortgage off over 15 years, so why keep it longer and pay that much more interest to the bank?

While I agree that the interest difference is large, if he had a 30-year mortgage, the monthly payments would be much smaller and he could either use that money to have a better quality of life, or he could put that money toward another investment. As long as that other investment had a higher return than the mortgage, he would make a profit. In Aaron's particular scenario, the profit could potentially be over one million dollars. If Aaron invests in anything with returns higher than his mortgage, he would be making money off the bank's money. This concept is called **positive carry**.

Backstage Glossary

Positive Carry: Making a profit on the difference between interest paid and investment earnings. For example, a difference between the interest you are paying on a loan (5%) vs the profit you receive investing those dollars elsewhere (8%) would result in a positive carry (3%).

There is also the issue of inflation. As prices go up over time, a dollar will purchase less. Borrowing money today and paying that same amount back later on, when the dollar's value is less, can be a smart strategy. This will have a more significant impact over 30 years vs 15.

After discussing this with Aaron many times, he told me that he's starting to change his perspective on things. He's not 100 percent there yet, but I think he will get there someday soon.

No matter how old you are, you aren't getting any younger

Life happens. Do you want to be able to do all the things you dream of doing right now? Or do you want to wait 15 to 30 years? I enjoy travel but I'm not sure I will be able to do as much traveling in 15 to 30 years. I probably won't have as much energy then as I do now. And what if something horrific happens to me before then? I could have a serious injury. I could die.

To be clear, and at the risk of sounding redundant, I am not championing some YOLO, go-for-broke approach to life; you will never catch me jumping out of an airplane or dangling from a bridge with a bungee cord attached to my leg. But I do know that nothing in life is certain and living a lifestyle you enjoy today is important—as long as you do it responsibly.

This is what I learned about taking your shot. It's never just one shot. It's the first in a series of steps that will ultimately lead you to where you want to go. But until you take that first shot, that first step, you will never take the second or the third or fourth.

I was on my way, learning a lot, and letting each step inform the next on my journey to financial freedom. And as I was about to discover, the road to destiny always involves a few wrong turns.

CHAPTER 6 LESSONS LEARNED

- Unlike birthdays, surprises in real estate are not generally happy occasions. Know what you are buying and know who your partners are.

- Not all prime markets are located in your backyard. Don't be afraid to cast about for the right market, even if you don't live there.

- Bargains can wind up more expensive than paying full price. Generally speaking, you get what you pay for. There are no real get rich-quick-schemes, and no free lunch.

- Not all workshops and real estate methods are created equal, so investigate before you invest, in education or property.

- Being financially free is not the same thing as being free from debt.

- Master your real estate fundamentals. More knowledge is always a good thing.

A WRONG TURN
IN ALBUQUERQUE

When you start looking to scale up your real estate investing, it can be difficult at first to find your way. An important concept I learned at the top is that there are essentially two ways to invest in real estate. You can be an active investor, or you can be a passive investor. Here is a little bit about both.

Active Investment

When you are an active investor, you do everything—and I mean everything—on your own. Most people become active investors when they buy a house. Thanks to my experiences with the Woodridge Lake house, I had a pretty good idea of what it means to build and then manage a rental property in addition to owning my own home. I had to find my own deal, forge my own relationships, build my community of trust, underwrite my deal, and on top of all that, I had to be my own property manager. That doesn't even include staying on top of financials and tax filings. And after all of that, I barely broke even.

I did get better at the process over time, with the Brooklyn property and house flips in Ohio, but I wondered if there was a way to scale up active investing in a way that made all that extra work pay off. In the meantime, I decided to spend some time learning more about passive investment.

Passive Investment

Compared to active investing, passive investment sounded like a cakewalk to me, although you do have to do your homework on the front end. You need to vet the deal and the people who are running it. You want to make sure you are in good hands. Once you know that, you can sit back and let the deal do what the deal does, leaving you with more time to focus on family, hobbies, and your other passions, while still being involved in profitable real estate deals. Hopefully this means there are profits coming back to you, if that the deal turns out to be a good one.

This sounded super attractive to me. I loved the idea of sitting back, relaxing, and making money while I sleep. I began to look into passive investment in a deeper and more specific way to find a path that might work for me. I found there were essentially two choices: funds and individual syndications.

Funds

In this scenario, you invest in a fund. They take your money and invest it in multiple properties that are packaged together. If you have ever heard of a REIT (Real Estate Investment Trust) they operate in a similar fashion, and they often invest in funds. Some types of investments have stated criteria, but often they are a "blind pool," which means that you are investing in the fund or REIT without knowing the details of the individual investments. The specific investments that the fund makes are selected by its leadership, which you, hopefully, trust implicitly, because you won't see the particulars on any deal before the fund invests in it.

Individual Syndications

Finally—and I saved the best for last—you can passively invest in real estate via a **syndication**. These are private offerings involving a group of people who are raising private equity to go after a property together. A syndication allows you to partner with other investors to aggregate capital and leverage the team's experience and financial strength to invest in otherwise unobtainable assets. The whole is truly greater than the sum of its parts!

Backstage Glossary

Syndication: The pooling of capital and resources among multiple investors to achieve a common goal.

Many, if not most, apartment complexes are bought through syndications. So are many other things like business properties, shopping centers, hotels, self-storage facilities, and even Broadway shows. You can come together with like-minded people and buy anything you want as a syndication. I loved this idea. I had always wanted to go bigger with my investments but lacked the ability to do this on my own. By pooling the resources of many investors together, what seemed out of reach could now be attainable through a syndication.

Don't lane hop, find your sweet spot and stay there for a while

Now that I had discovered my sweet spot, I wanted to learn more, to know everything there was to know about syndication. That's the kind of a guy I am, voracious when it comes to background research. I started working on my new major at Podcast University and consumed everything I could find online. Just like my old days at AMDA, or the year I spent locked in my apartment learning how to code, I devoured everything I could about real estate syndication.

When you start looking into syndications you really have to know a lot of things that can be very tedious to learn. First, it's good to have a basic knowledge of the **SEC** requirements. Second, the financial gate is high, the deals can be complex, and as I've come to understand, the devil is always in the details.

> ## Backstage Glossary
>
> **SEC:** The Securities and Exchange Commission (SEC) was created following the 1929 stock market crash. It is a part of the federal government that protects investors.

This is why I have included "A Backstage Tour of Syndications" at the back of the book, where I provide all of the fine points—the tedious stuff that I learned from podcasts, seminars, classrooms, and from my own personal experience—that you absolutely have to know. It doesn't make for a very scintillating read, and it runs parallel to the main story, but you'll need to familiarize yourself with the nitty gritty if you are ready to get serious. It's much harder to learn as you go, like I did in Albuquerque, as you're about to see in just a little bit.

I found an in-person workshop promising to teach everything you need to know about syndication. A few weeks later, I flew to Texas and entered a ballroom at the Westin Hotel in Dallas for my first syndication workshop. There were about 100 other investors there. All of them were interested in syndication, most of them had already done at least a deal or two, and several were **sponsors.**

> ### Backstage Glossary
>
> **Sponsor:** A person who leads a syndication or partnership. They may also be called a "syndicator" or "general partner." There is often more than one sponsor on a deal. They can have different roles ranging from the identification and acquisition of properties, through the operation and ultimate disposition of the property.

My eyes opened wide as we went around the room and everyone introduced themselves and stated how many units they owned. I was amazed that there were several people whose experience matched my own and so many had done far more than I had. I have to say, I was impressed. I was sure I was in the right place.

Hundreds of thousands of units were represented in this room. I met amazing people with fantastic backgrounds, all at different stages of their real estate journeys. I met people that day who are now close personal friends and professional colleagues. Making connections like these are crucial to success and I learned a lot about my newly adopted strategy for building my real estate empire.

At the end of the workshop, I was presented with the opportunity to enroll in a more intensive program. It was, of course, also way more expensive. I passed on that opportunity but walked away from that experience with a clear vision. I wanted to use the syndication model and focus on apartments.

At the recommendation of a few of my new real estate friends from that first syndication workshop, I attended a different workshop a few months later that was focused specifically on apartment syndication. This time, when the inevitable higher ticket item came up again, I really thought hard about making the commitment. The cost was a lot of money for me at that time. Outside of the down payment on a piece of property, this would be the single largest check I had ever written!

I talked to my wife about the opportunity. I had saved money over the years before we even met, so technically the funds I would use to pay for this were "mine," but I certainly wanted her buy-in, and she was supportive. I also called my mom and dad. I think they thought I was being conned. They knew I was serious and smart and they knew they had taught me well, but they were skeptical, thinking I was spending a lot of money on something that would ultimately be impossible to accomplish. But I was pretty sure of myself. This wasn't a no-money-down, get-rich-quick scheme. It would take a lot of time and effort, I would need my own capital and the ability to raise more from others to make this happen. It felt like a real opportunity and I felt like I was ready for the challenge.

Invest in your own education, it's so worth it

I've done quite a few of these workshops and seminars and I have learned a lot about them, some good, some bad. Bottom line: the advantage to join-ing one of these programs is that you collapse time-frames. They provide a mentor or coach, someone with a proven track record who can show you the ropes and help you avoid mistakes—many of which they may have made along the way—so you don't have to. Apartment complexes are high-ticket items. Learning how to avoid just one mistake can pay for the entire mentorship program. At least that's what I was telling myself at the time. And I wasn't far off. Joining one of these programs was one of the best decisions I made for my career, but was not something I did lightly.

KEYSTONE CONCEPT #10
Don't Be Afraid of Gurus

Having a mentor or coach, someone who's been there before, can collapse time frames and save you a lot of costly mistakes. Just keep your eyes open and remember to trust but verify.

I distinctly remember when I made the final decision to join the program. It was early on a Monday morning after the seminar and I was at the DFW airport, about to fly back home. I was at the gate waiting for the plane to board, talking to my friend Chris. I had met Chris a few months back at the first seminar in Dallas. He was in the program I was about to join and I knew he didn't always see eye-to-eye with the program's leader. This was a good thing, as I believed he would give me an honest opinion about the program. I remember my heart racing as I told him that it was a huge amount of money for me to spend. I was literally sweating. Was I being conned out of tens of thousands of dollars? Would *this* be Matt's Folly?

Chris told me that he had gotten a lot out of the program. He had passively invested in several deals as a result and had even sponsored a deal, so he was on his way to making more than his money back. He assured me that spending such a large sum of money on any program really said something about who I was and what I was committing to. He said that if he had learned anything about me it was that I don't spend my money foolishly or take my commitments lightly. He thought that if I put that type of money down on the program, I would be making a commitment to myself to get tremendous value out of it and that I would be successful. For better or worse, I bought his reasoning. I resolved that if I put my money in, I would find a way to earn my money back, and I plunked my nest egg down.

Don't jump at the first deal that comes along

Right away, new opportunities began presenting themselves through all these connections I was making at seminars. I attended one seminar where I met a fairly well-known syndicator who had done a number of deals. In discussions with him, I learned that he sometimes put together groups of current and potential investors to go to a city where he invests to learn about that market and see his properties. A couple of months later, I received an email invitation to one of his market trips. I decided to join the trip as this would be a great opportunity for several reasons.

First and foremost, I was genuinely interested in making my first passive investment and I thought this was potentially a great fit. Secondly, it was an opportunity to learn about a new market; observing how this person analyzes markets could be a good learning opportunity. Lastly, I wanted to see how he ran his syndications and his business along with how he put together events. I had a lot to learn and nothing to lose, so I signed up.

I had a nice couple of days in that city and met some great people, but ultimately I chose not to invest in that person's deals. I had some fairly basic, straightforward questions about the deals and the operations of the properties, and I was very surprised that he, as the sponsor, couldn't answer my questions. He deferred to the property management company and I found that their answers weren't satisfying either.

These were big red flags for me. You have to be comfortable with the sponsor on a deal, and I wasn't feeling certain. In addition, when we toured his properties, they were all in terrible shape: hallways, stairwells, exteriors, and interiors were all a mess. These weren't newly acquired properties, he had owned some of them for years, and they were still, essentially, in shambles.

Don't get me wrong, I knew these were going to be **Class C** properties, so I wasn't expecting luxurious digs, but still, these properties were in unbelievably bad shape and more like **Class D**. I felt bad for the people who lived there and was unsure about being involved. This sponsor had a reputation for being successful though, and I really wanted to invest in a syndication. I thought long and hard about this and about myself. What were my goals and aspirations? What did I stand for? What types of initiatives did I want to put my money behind? Ultimately, I came to the inevitable conclusion that this deal was not for me. My investment philosophy didn't mesh with the syndicator's, a very important consideration in any deal.

> ## Backstage Glossary
>
> **Property Classes (A, B, C & D):** A non-standard classification of properties based on the age of their construction and current condition. While there is no specific set of rules, they are generally grouped as: Class A being constructed within the last 10 years, in great condition, and a top-notch set of amenities. Class B properties are 10 to 30 years old, in good condition, and in good locations. Class C Properties are 30 years or older with a greater need for repairs and maintenance and are generally located in less affluent areas. Class D properties are also 30 years or older but have a significant amount of deferred maintenance and are often located in high crime areas.

These investments might have made me a large pile of cash, but it was clear to me that those profits were at the expense of the tenants who had to live there. By cutting expenses as far as possible, you can make a nice profit, but the residents at the property suffer. I got into the real estate game to make money, but I also remembered the story in the musical *Rent*. I was not getting involved to become Benny. I was going to make a difference. I wanted to be an investor who made the world better for everyone. I had meant that when I said it, and I was using that as my North Star. I decided right then and there that my goals, investment philosophy, and values need to match those of the people I choose to do business with.

After this trip, what I was looking for became clearer to me because I had learned what I wasn't looking for. I also discovered that I had developed a pretty good working knowledge of my sector. I actually knew what I was doing! And I even understood some of the mechanics of real estate better than the property manager and sponsor I had been talking to. I knew I could run a property better than these people. I felt certain I could find projects where there was an opportunity to improve the residents' lives *and* make a profit as well. I wanted a win-win approach. That was my path.

Unicorns are a mythical beast

As the plane touched down on my next flight to Dallas, I took out my cell phone to text Erica and let her know I'd arrived safely. This had become my routine with all my traveling. As we taxied to the terminal, my phone lit up with multiple emails from my friend Chris. Chris had just got a deal that he was sponsoring! I couldn't wait to get off the plane and call him. I was about to run headlong into my first syndication opportunity.

"I've got an amazing opportunity," Chris told me excitedly. "It's a complex in Albuquerque. The deal terms are amazing and so are my partners. I'm going in with a couple of friends, Franklin and Clara. You'll love them, they're great."

Hmm, I thought to myself. Albuquerque, New Mexico—a town I knew of from childhood only because Bugs Bunny was always making a wrong turn there. I couldn't stop thinking about what Chris had told me though. When I got to the hotel, I sent him an email congratulating him and letting him know I was looking forward to hearing more. I was in town for an apartment complex bus tour and networking event. The next day, on the bus, I sat with Chris and he told me all about it. This was incredible! Coming in as a passive investor in a deal that Chris and his friends were sponsoring couldn't have sounded more ideal. I was walking on sunshine.

I reviewed the underwriting on the deal, which all made sense to me. It followed the model we had all been taught in the mentorship group. Chris and the others had even gone over the deal with our mentor as well as some other very experienced investors. Everything seemed to check out. More attractive than the underwriting, though, was the level of trust I had in Chris.

I knew him pretty well by then, and I liked him a lot. Chris was a Navy pilot turned commercial airline captain and I trusted his judgment. He was careful, he was thorough, and like a pilot, he had checklists for everything to make sure every detail was accounted for before takeoff. While he was relatively new to sponsoring deals, I felt he would be a good steward of my capital and that, if things went wrong, I could count on him to fight as hard as he needed to, to make sure things turned out okay. If he could land a 757, I knew he could land this deal.

I was becoming aware of another of my guiding pillars in my investment philosophy: I need to be absolutely comfortable with the deal sponsor. So comfortable, in fact, that I would sometimes be my own sponsor, but that was still down the road. Right now, I wanted more than anything to invest, and invest with a sponsor I could trust. Chris was that guy.

Smaller is not necessarily better when it comes to minimum investments

$50,000 was the minimum investment in this deal. Minimums in deals are usually between $50,000– $100,000. I've seen small offerings with $25,000 minimums but those are rare. Early on I was looking for $25,000 minimums or asking sponsors if I could get in at $25,000. Now I realize this wasn't a great idea. The scale of the returns on these vs the effort and your own administrative expenses aren't great, so I find it better to invest in larger amounts if possible.

Put your retirement savings to work for you now but be careful

I was able to do the investment with money I had accumulated in my 401(k). I'd always been a little frustrated with my 401(k) and IRAs as my investment options were always limited to the funds that the custodian offered. When I was younger, I'd thought that was great because I didn't need to do any research; I just put my money in and it grew by the percentage shown in the prospectus. Over time, I learned that this wasn't the case. Certain funds perform, some over perform, and some underperform.

In times of economic crisis, I would watch my balance sink and then take many years to recover. A 50% market loss requires a 100% gain just to get back to even! Once a year I would sit down with my financial advisor and review everything. And every year I was disappointed with what I felt was dismal growth.

Through my research I discovered that I could move my money into a Self-Directed IRA (**SDIRA**). I rolled over some of my retirement funds into a SDIRA, where you have a lot more options as to what you can do with your money. You can invest in almost anything you want: mutual funds, individual stocks, or other things like Broadway musicals or real estate syndications. It sounded perfect, just like this deal.

Backstage Glossary

SDIRA: A Self-Directed Individual Retirement Account is an account that can hold a variety of alternative investments normally unavailable in an IRA. Although the account is administered by a custodian or trustee, it's directly managed by the account holder—the reason it's called self-directed.

Unfortunately, a few months into this syndication I discovered that I didn't understand the regulations on the SDIRA thoroughly. I found out I was going to get hit with a large tax bill at the sale of the property. It turns out there is a lesser-known thing called **UBIT**, which is a tax that is applied to gains inside a SDIRA if those gains are from borrowed money. Essentially, if you invest in a real estate deal that has a 75% loan, then you will be subject to tax on 75% of your gain. There are types of Qualified Retirement Plans (**QRP**s) that can help you avoid UBIT but I didn't know about them back then. What a rude awakening for me when I found out about the tax bill I would have to pay on my first real estate transaction in my SDIRA. Not my happiest day. And that wasn't the only rude awakening on my "perfect" first deal.

> ### Backstage Glossary
>
> **UBIT:** Unrelated Business Income Tax is tax that is imposed on a tax-exempt organization that is not related to the tax-exempt purpose of that organization. If you invest in a property that utilizes debt (a mortgage), then you may be subject to tax on the gains attributed to that mortgage. For example, if a property is purchased with a 75% mortgage, then 75% of your gains are subject to tax.
>
> **QRP:** A Qualified Retirement Plan, recognized by the IRS, where your money can grow with special tax advantages. Taxes can be deferred, or in the case of a Roth, your money can grow tax free. Most plans offered from an employer, like a 401(k), are qualified plans.

Question all assumptions

The paperwork for the Albuquerque deal was overwhelming, and I wanted to actually read all of it before I signed. But looking at my first investment, with no experience having done these before, I missed a few things. Chris's friends Franklin and Clara had put together a nice investor packet with information on the sponsors, the market, and the deal, which all appealed to me. The sponsors seemed like nice people from the Sun Belt. And then there was Navy pilot Chris. I mean, what could go wrong? The answer is, lots of things. I have since learned how to look under the hood to see what is driving those numbers and assumptions.

That is one of the big reasons I wrote this book: to teach people how to look under the hood and question assumptions.

Bottom line—these deals aren't easy to pull off. As someone who runs them regularly, I can tell you it takes a lot of work and a ton of asset management to make them successful. I find it challenging, even with my very conservative underwriting. So, when people have aggressive underwriting, if one little thing goes wrong, the whole project can be in big trouble.

KEYSTONE CONCEPT #11
A Deal Is Only as Strong as Your Team

Ensure that your project has a strong team with people who have experience operating large scale businesses. There is a big difference between drafting a business plan and actually executing it, and you need people on board who know what they are doing, especially at the beginning.

It took me all weekend to get through over 100 pages of documentation on the Albuquerque project. My eyes crossed and I fell asleep a few times but I made it through at last. I actually appreciated the documentation, and once I had gotten past the legalese, it was all extremely helpful. It clearly laid out all the deal points and the way everything would be run. It was all there in black and white, as if Chris had written one of his famous checklists, so the reader could fully understand what they were getting into, how the company would be run, and the way the company would handle all possible scenarios.

"Okay, I've decided. I want to invest in the deal," I told Chris at last. "One thing though. I'm going to look at this as a learning opportunity. So, I'll probably call with questions from time to time. Is that Okay?"

"Of course, that's okay," Chris said. "I wouldn't expect anything less. I know you want to sponsor your own deals in the future and we're happy to answer your questions. I'm so glad you'll be joining us. You won't be sorry, and you are going to learn a lot."

I signed the paperwork, wired the funds, and that's how I became the happy owner of an apartment complex in Albuquerque. I was a passive investor, so I got an email letting me know when we closed on the purchase of the property. Everything was done, and that, as they say, was that.

I remember how proud and excited I was the day we closed on the property. I posted a picture of the property on Facebook thanking the sponsors for putting together the deal and gushing about how proud I was to be investing in the project. My Facebook lit up like a Christmas tree with my friends congratulating me and telling me I was a real estate mogul now! I kind of felt like a titan for a brief moment, but I didn't believe the hype. I knew I was just starting out and had much to learn. This is a good attitude to maintain throughout your investment career. I learned it as an actor: never believe your own reviews.

A couple of months into the operation of the property, I received the first monthly report. I took a look at the financials. Everything seemed to look fine, only there were a number of line items in the profit and loss statement that I didn't understand.

Line items in the P&L aren't the most descriptive; for the uninitiated they can be mysterious. I was pretty sure that NSF wasn't a donation to the National Science Foundation (turns out it's a rent payment that was returned for insufficient funds). I figured this was a good time to learn something I didn't know and sent an email to the sponsors asking for a call to explain things to me.

A deal sponsor is the person (or people) in charge of everything on the deal, and this includes reviewing the financials regularly. If the sponsor can't review those statements reliably, there is a *big* issue because they are supposed to be going over them with the property manager each month to make sure the business is being run efficiently. It's also up to the deal sponsor to ensure that the property management team isn't stealing from you.

Franklin responded to my email and we set up a phone call to go over the financials and learn what I didn't know.

As we were going through the P&L statement line by line, I realized he didn't know much more than I did about the line items I was questioning. That was shocking. Some of them were easy, like "rental income" or "vacancy." No problem. But each time we got to one that I didn't understand (like "NSF"), it seemed he didn't know what it was either.

After this happened a few times, I started to get an uneasy feeling. Why the heck was this guy running the deal? He didn't understand this stuff. We were a few months into the deal at this point. He should have been reviewing these financials regularly. He'd been sending them to us, saying they were reviewed and giving us a report. But then, when it came to the details, he was clueless. How does that work? It didn't add up for me. Something didn't feel right.

After that call, I sent a follow up email to the whole team. I was polite but I said I was expecting another call with details on these items. That's when Chris jumped in. We got on a call and he was able to explain to me every line item in detail. We also spoke about the operations and how everything was going. We must have been on the phone for over 90 minutes. That was the beginning of Chris and I forging a deeper relationship. From then on, we had long and pretty deep calls. Still to this day, we can talk for hours.

Despite how well Chris and I hit it off, this deal was going off-track. Our occupancy was unbelievably low, month after month. They couldn't get the property functioning well. I was freaking out. I had $50,000 tied up in this deal. It seemed certain I was going to lose it all. This *was* Matt's Folly after all!

I had settled on Chris as my point person because he was the only one who seemed to understand what he was doing, and I watched as he went into "pilot in an emergency" mode, working day and night to land the injured plane.

I was pushing Chris to sell the property for about a year before they actually did. My theory was that **cap rates** and interest rates were still low but looked like they might start rising and that we should sell the property and get out while we could still come close to breaking even. We were in a loan that had interest-only payments for the first few years (this is common) but once we would have to start making principal payments as well, it would kill us. We had no free cash flow and received no distributions. My unicorn investment had turned into a scruffy and obstinate donkey.

> ## Backstage Glossary
>
> **Cap Rate:** The abbreviation of Capitalization Rate. A metric used to evaluate different pieces of real estate under the same terms so as to be able to make an "apples to apples" comparison. Cap rates remove the financing component and assume that a property is purchased on an all-cash basis. This way, investors understand a property's performance regardless of financing, since it can drastically change the risks and returns of a deal, depending on many factors such as interest rate, amount of leverage, and length of the loan etc. Cap rate levels the playing field so deals can be compared from an equal starting point.

On our calls, Chris detailed all the tactics they were employing to turn the property around. They were having weekly calls with the property management team. Eventually they fired the incompetent property management company and brought in a new team. They did some upgrades and tried to build a better sense of community in the building to attract residents. They did a big project to generate press where they hired a local artist to paint a mural on the side of the building. Everyone in town was able to be involved by throwing balloons of paint against the wall to create a colorful background for the painting. They had local news coverage in print and TV for the event. They installed a fence around the property to add more of a sense of security and safety.

Chris tried everything he could think of, we literally exhausted the list of options, and then tried a few more. Still, in the end, nothing worked. If you get into a bad situation in a bad location and you are that far off on your rent projections, no amount of work or creative problem solving is going to bail you out. But sometimes, you'll get a stroke of good luck, that turns everything around. A get out of jail free card. This time, that's what happened for us. There was a buyer who needed to do a **1031 exchange** and somehow was convinced to buy our property at a price where we eked out a small profit.

Backstage Glossary

1031 Exchange: This allows you to defer (*not eliminate*) paying taxes on the profits from a sale of property provided you purchase a similar property of equal or greater value. There are strict guidelines and timing requirements that must be adhered to in order to utilize this tax deferment strategy. The name comes from Section 1031 of the U.S. Tax Code where the rules for it are defined, but it is also known as a "Like Kind Exchange" or "Tax Deferred Exchange."

While the profit was minuscule, I was relieved we didn't lose money in the deal. I give all the credit for saving it to Chris, because without his Herculean efforts, we would have lost a lot. Chris would not let that happen. This was a real-life lesson for me on the critical importance of having a strong sponsor on any deal.

Sponsors can be your best friend or your worst enemy

You can think of a deal sponsor like the CEO of a company. A talented CEO can lead a company to greatness, while a poor leader can be the cause of a great company's demise. Regardless of the deal itself, if the sponsor can't run it well, it can lose money. Conversely, if a deal starts going south, a strong sponsor can save it. We had a flawed business plan on the Albuquerque property, but Chris, as a sponsor on the deal, worked tirelessly to keep us airborne and bring us in for a safe landing.

I learned from this experience that there are three things you need to look at when you're vetting a syndication: the market, the deal, and most importantly, the sponsors. We will deal with the other two in the next chapters, but this story is a cautionary tale about the crucial role of the deal sponsor. What the Albuquerque deal taught me is that you need to look first and foremost at the sponsor who is running the deal: that makes all the difference.

KEYSTONE CONCEPT #12
The Three Deal Pillars

The three pillars that you need to evaluate when sizing up any deal are: The Sponsor, The Market, and The Deal. The most important one is the sponsor.

You can have a fantastic deal in a fantastic market but if the team that's running it doesn't know what they're doing, it can go south very quickly. Make sure you vet whomever you're working with very carefully as you are going to be investing tens or maybe hundreds of thousands of dollars of your hard-earned cash.

Make sure your sponsor is going to be a good steward of your capital. Take a look at their background and their experience when it comes to real estate and managing finances. I'm not suggesting that you shouldn't give someone an opportunity, even the most successful people had to start somewhere. But especially if it's the first time you're investing in a syndication, I would recommend that you go with someone with experience. Their experience doesn't necessarily have to all be in real estate syndications. Maybe they've had a parallel experience in a different industry.

When looking at the sponsorship team, find out what sort of track record they have—what other deals they've done and how those deals have performed. If you can get references from a few other people that have invested with them, that's great, but obtaining those references can be difficult and awkward. Sponsors can be reluctant to give out the names of their investors, who are usually very busy professionals.

My favorite way to meet a sponsor is to be introduced by another investor that I trust. That way, I know they vouch for the sponsor. I find that's the best way to have confidence in someone you haven't worked with before. If a friend of mine tells me they worked with a sponsor and that sponsor was great, very communicative, and kept them informed through the whole process (and by the way, made a handsome profit) then that is someone I want to meet!

Talk turkey with your sponsor right from the top

As a passive investor, I want to work with a sponsor who matches my communication style, has similar goals, the same approach to project management, and common values. Having a conversation about these things at the beginning can give you an understanding of the sponsor and how they handle their deals.

How is everything going to be run? How communicative are they going to be? How frequently will they communicate? Are they going to send out monthly updates? Quarterly updates? Are you only going to get an update when there's bad news? Will they devote the time to actually get on the phone with you if you have questions? If you have concerns, will they discuss things with you? Transparency and accessibility are two of the things that I look for most in a sponsor. I want to know I'm investing with someone I can get ahold of, and who will answer questions when I have them.

A great way to test a sponsor's communication and openness/transparency is to watch how the exchange goes at the beginning. Are they easy to deal with? Are they able to get on the phone and talk you through the deal from start to finish? How do they act when they're on the phone with you? When you ask questions or challenge assumptions, how do they react? If they aren't available and transparent before you invest, how are they going to behave once you've already given them your money?

A discussion about what really matters to you at the top is important. It will help you get a good feel for the person and how they're going to react during the rest of the deal. If they're not very helpful at the beginning when they're trying to get you to invest, it's not going to get any better from there on out.

SEC rules are not made to be broken

A big red flag for me is when a sponsor doesn't follow SEC rules. These are the important regulations that you need to pay attention to.

You will run into many in the business who are willing to split the difference or skirt around the margins when it comes to regulations. Much of that may be harmless, but you have to ask yourself if you want to give your money to someone with that attitude. You might go ahead and decide to invest in that deal anyway. If the deal goes well, probably nothing bad will happen, because it's unlikely that anyone is going to reach out to the SEC and complain about rules being broken, so it flies under the radar.

I would urge you, however, to question whether you want to do business with this person. Someone who is breaking the law or "bending the rules" may very well be doing the same thing in other aspects of their business. I don't think that bodes well for that sponsor.

The same is true when working with someone who is qualifying their investors. A sponsor is not allowed to bring unaccredited investors into certain types of deals. But I have heard of sponsors saying things like, "it looks like you're almost an **accredited investor**, so I'll let you in the deal." Besides opening themselves up to a potential liability, what other things are they letting slide? Maybe something in the underwriting? Maybe the exit cap rate? Maybe the rental growth? If a sponsor is being loose here and there, these things add up, and next thing you know, their deal is not as strong as you are being led to believe. Look at the integrity of the person and whether they are bending the rules. This is important.

Backstage Glossary

Accredited Investor: A person with an individual or joint net worth (with a spouse) of more than $1 million, excluding their primary residence. Or, someone who in each of the last two years has had an individual income in excess of $200,000—or a joint income (with a spouse) in excess of $300,000—and reasonably expects to continue to reach that income level. As of August 2020, the SEC also defined measures of professional knowledge, experience, or certifications in addition to the tests for income or net worth.

This leads to one last important thing—don't get involved with a sponsor who is solely raising capital. There are many people out there who want to get involved just to raise capital and become a general partner in the deal. This happens all the time. According to the rules and regulations set forth by the SEC however, you cannot solely raise capital on a deal. This is something I've heard SEC attorneys talk about many times at seminars and on podcasts. It is a violation of the SEC rules. A sponsor's compensation cannot be based on the amount of capital they raise. If someone is raising money for a deal and that is all they are doing, they are breaking the rules.

Each member of the general partnership team must have legitimate duties beyond just raising capital. Obviously capital must be raised to have the equity needed to close the deal, and there's nothing wrong with that. But if that is someone's only role in the deal, then that's illegal. This speaks to the integrity of the syndicator. If you know the syndicator is solely raising capital, are they knowingly breaking the law? If so, that's a big red flag. If they don't know it's not allowed, that's a bigger red flag. In either case, is this someone you want to trust with your money?

Find a sponsor who is actually in charge

I want to know that the sponsor who I'm talking with on the phone is truly a general partner. I want to know that my sponsors are decision makers. Do they only have a small percentage in a deal? Do they have a seat at the table when large decisions are being made? Most of the time, people who are just raising capital don't have a seat at the table, and they're lucky if they can even listen in on phone calls here and there. They're not part of that decision-making process. That's a problem.

When I'm investing in a deal, I'm trusting that person with my money. Their partners are an important part of the team, but my chief concern is the sponsor I'm investing through. Who am I actually speaking with and what is their role in the organization? That's important to understand. I want to be clear on whether I'm dealing with a lead person who's really running the deal or if they only play a minor role. I want to understand what their level of influence is in the decisions that are being made.

A polished and professional presence is important

I also look at a sponsor's website and the marketing materials when considering a deal. As someone who was in digital marketing for many years, I have a particular interest in this. It's not the most important thing when considering an investment, but I do want to invest with someone who comes across as professional. It doesn't need to be flashy, but I want to do business with someone who has a nice website and a professional investor presentation that looks clean, is visually appealing, and is not riddled with typos.

For me, attention to detail speaks volumes for how this sponsorship team is going to manage the deal. If these first things are sloppy, my experience has shown me that the deal is run with equal disregard. I want to know that they actually have a business card, a domain name, and a real business email, not "smartinvestor242@gmail.com."

Long story short, knowing who is running your deal and going through a checklist of the things about that person that matter to you is crucial in selecting investments that are going to work for you long term.

$$\bowtie$$

CHAPTER 7 LESSONS LEARNED

- Mentors and mentorship programs can help collapse time frames and save you money, time, and headaches.

- Invest in your education. Even as a passive investor, you should still have a minimum level of knowledge before participating in someone else's deal.

- Look for the red flags early and often before committing your investment. You have more leverage before you invest than after.

- A strong sponsor can save a flawed business plan but a weak sponsor can ruin a perfect business plan.

- Invest with people you know, like, and trust.

- Invest with people who have an investment philosophy aligned with your core values and beliefs.

CHAPTER 8

CHARTING A COURSE TO FINANCIAL FREEDOM

Afer my initial investment in the Albuquerque deal, I continued investing passively in other syndications. I was trying to put the lessons I was learning to good use and not to make the same mistakes twice. I was careful with whom I invested, making sure it was people I knew, liked, and trusted.

I was also purposely investing with different syndicators. I wanted to do this for two reasons. The first was to diversify my real estate holdings. Just like the advice you'd get from a financial advisor looking at your investments, I wanted to have my holdings in different places. In case one didn't perform well, the others might make up for that. I wanted to have my investments spread across different markets and different operators.

The second reason was that I knew I wanted to sponsor deals on my own, and by investing across these different operators I was able to see how they approached deals and how they operated them. I got to witness firsthand how they overcame challenges, the types of communication and reporting they provided, and much more. I knew I'd learn a lot and would be able to pull out the best-in-class options and incorporate them into how I did business.

You won't really own your goals until you write them down

I was never a guy who wrote down my goals. I always figured I knew what I wanted to do and I'd figure out how to get there. I'd do whatever it took to learn everything I needed to learn to make it happen. I'm a driven person. During my years at the management level in corporate America, I found myself mentoring teams, helping them develop goals that were written down and evaluated on a yearly basis. These were mandated, and I had to write them for myself as well. We made sure our goals were SMART, which stands for Specific, Measurable, Attainable, Relevant, and Time-Bound.

KEYSTONE CONCEPT #13
Write Down Your Goals

Set goals and then write them down. Writing them down helps you to understand your mission in a deeper way. The list will serve as a good way to check in with yourself, keep focused, and measure your progress.

Over time, I've changed my mind about writing down goals. I've realized throughout my career and in working with others, that those who set goals and write them down and are able to check their progress periodically tend to perform better than people who don't. I recommend that everyone do the same, even though it might feel out of character.

Create a road map for success

As an Excel nerd who loves spreadsheets, I felt that putting my real estate goals down in pixels would be a good way for me to track my progress and keep myself accountable. I wanted a road map I could follow. Here is how I started charting a road forward, on my computer.

First, I remembered that Robert Kiyosaki mentioned that it's a good idea to start tracking your **net worth**, so I decided to start there. I had a **PFS** (Personal Financial Statement) spreadsheet given to me by a mortgage broker. PFSs are used when applying for a commercial loan: they detail all your assets and liabilities, tally them, and show your net worth. The first time I did one of these it felt kind of weird. I'll admit it did bring to mind Scrooge McDuck, in his vault with mountains of gold. But I realized that this is just a barometer, a score card that banks require in order to lend you money. I remember doing a scaled down version of one of these when I applied for mortgages for my personal residences in the past. I completed my first PFS and tracked my progress every six months or so. This was a great first step, and I recommend it as a place to start.

> **Backstage Glossary**
>
> **Net Worth:** The sum total of everything you own (all your assets) minus everything you owe (all your liabilities).
>
> **PFS:** Your Personal Financial Statement details all of your assets and liabilities. This is required by most lenders in order to get a mortgage; it can provide a clear and concise picture of all your finances.

From there, I created a passive investment spreadsheet, which was very basic at the beginning. I started with a yearly projection for the few real estate investments I had at the time: the Brooklyn property, a couple of turnkey single-family properties, and a syndication. It didn't add up to very much passive income at the start.

This spreadsheet has now evolved into something I call my "investment tracker." It is my dashboard, the most important document I have from a passive investment perspective. It's a multi-tabbed spreadsheet that contains a 15-year plan. It shows all the investments I have made along with those I plan to make and their projected returns. I use it to track all the investments I make and how they perform, and I use the historical performance data to help evaluate future investment opportunities.

Don't expect your map to be this detailed at the beginning. This kind of complexity evolves over time. Here is what you can ask yourself to help you create one of your own. Essentially, it all boils down to three big questions:

- Where am I now?
- Where do I want to go?
- How do I get there?

Where am I now?

Just like I listed all my investments, you will want to list all of the income streams you can currently count on that you can invest into deals now and in the future. How much of the income from your job can you save to put into investments? Will you receive any increases to your salary or bonuses? What else can you do to generate capital to invest? Do you have any skills you can utilize to create income? Do you have anything you can sell? Can you comfortably refinance your property? Have you looked into a self-directed IRA? Anything else? Air rights? Inheritance?

If you have an investment that is giving you a return, include that. If you have $100,000 in a syndication deal that is supposed to give you a 10% return, include that $10k for every year of the investment. Also remember to include the expected return at the sale of the property several years from now. This is a living document, if that investment doesn't give you the expected returns, that's okay, you can adjust it in your spreadsheet over time.

Where do I want to go?

Next, you need to determine where you want to be. How much passive income are you trying to generate? Are you looking to grow a retirement fund? Pay for your kid's education? Build a dream vacation home? Create a charitable organization? You need to define your destination before you can plan the way to get there.

My ultimate goal was to become "financially free." To me, this meant creating a life where my family (Erica, myself, and our two daughters) could enjoy a nice lifestyle but without having to ever work at a traditional job. This isn't to say that we wouldn't do anything with our lives. Erica, for instance, loves her job, works with fantastic people, and will certainly continue to work in theater no matter what.

We want to be productive, but with the freedom to choose to do things that are meaningful to us beyond just our salaries. I want my family to be able to choose what we do, how we do it, and why.

How do I get there?

After determining where I wanted to be from a passive investment perspective, I was able to calculate the gap between where I was and where I wanted to be. I then carefully crafted a plan to achieve those goals. Doing an exercise like this, painful though it may be at the beginning, helps you determine how much capital you will need to invest to reach your goals.

Based on your starting capital, how much you can contribute and how those investments perform will dictate how many years it takes for you to hit your passive income number. Map out how much you will invest and how much those investments return over the next several years. Then re-invest those returns into additional investments. It will probably take a couple of hours to put this together. Once you map it all out, you can see how much you need to invest, at what rate of return, and for how many years, in order to reach your goal.

Over the years, my "investment tracker" has become a living document that I am constantly adjusting in real time. Road maps are never going to be static or rigid or carved in stone. These documents need to live and breathe with agility. You need to be able to change plans, sometimes on a dime. While you must always remember that things will change, having this road map will help you to keep track of your vision and measure your progress. I recommend that you update your progress on a monthly basis.

A plan is only as good as its execution

Once I completed my initial spreadsheet model, I needed to execute my plan. I continued all my networking activities at local meetups along with conferences, seminars, and mentorship groups across the U.S. Through these networking opportunities, I obtained access to a wide range of deals that I was able to analyze. This was great for me, because through these networking activities I received an invaluable education in what worked best for me and what didn't.

KEYSTONE CONCEPT #14

Your Network = Your Net Worth
Start close with family, then friends, then friends of friends. Your network needs to grow organically with you, so be sure to tend to it like a real estate bonsai tree.

There's that old saying that the three most important things in real estate are location, location, location. And I learned early on the truth behind those words. There are always exceptions to any rule, but I tended to invest in the middle of the country, which generally doesn't have the same volatility of higher priced coastal markets. While this approach may not be for everybody, for me—a relative beginner when I started out and a cautious person by nature—this worked best.

Develop a solid foundation for your analysis by keeping it local

I always start by reviewing the materials the sponsor has given me. There is usually some great information there, even though such materials are, of course, promotional by definition. As I've said, I put a lot of thought into vetting the deal sponsor and deciding whether or not I can rely on their character, their integrity, and their insight. I always spot-check a couple of data points to make sure the facts I'm being given are accurate. My policy is trust, but verify.

I tell investors that real estate is hyper-local. What do I mean by this? I mean drilling down deeper than just the general market. When talking about a market, there's a greater market area, such as the **MSA** (Metropolitan Statistical Area), and there will also be a specific submarket where the property is located: the particular area surrounding the property. While this is true in cities, areas can change quite drastically and very quickly in the suburbs too.

Backstage Glossary

MSA: The Metropolitan Statistical Area, a geographical area defined by the federal Office of Management and Budget (OMB) that represents the metropolitan area of a city.

The importance of thinking hyper-locally and drilling down, street corner by street corner, was something I learned from living in New York City where things shift radically block-by-block in terms of lifestyle and property values. At one end of a block, you can have a place that you would never walk by at night, and then at the other end of that block (or even in the middle of the block) you can have a luxury multi-million-dollar high rise. That was the case with our townhome in Brooklyn at the time we purchased it.

The submarket is the neighborhood where your property is located, and it can exert a dramatic influence on the property's performance. I make sure a sponsor has provided me with information not only on the broader market but the specific submarket as well.

For example, I have properties in Kansas City, which is a very large MSA. There are many different sections within Kansas City, which spans two states. One of my deals in Kansas City is located in Gladstone, Missouri. That's the submarket. When I prepared my presentation for investors, I included information on Kansas City as a whole and then drilled down to information on the specific Gladstone area, which covers approximately eight square miles. I then drilled down even further showing details on the one-mile, three-mile, and five-mile radius from the property. I like to zoom in close on the specific data of what's happening right there, right now, because these details matter, and the more focused you can get on the facts surrounding your specific location, the better prepared investors will be to make a well-informed decision.

Do the math

There are usually specific data points that I'm looking for on any property. They are important metrics that help me understand where the market is now and where it's going tomorrow, next month, next year. What is the current population and projected growth? What are the current economic drivers, and what is the diversity of those drivers? Does the local economy depend on one employer? If that employer goes out of business or moves their facility to another location, is that going to kill that submarket? Having employment diversity is really important. Think Flint, Michigan, when the automobile industry left—total devastation! I also look at things like local wages, crime rates, and schools—these are all very important.

One of the statistics I like to look at is the HHI (household income). By looking at the median HHI, I can see if it supports the pro forma rents that are in the underwriting. As a general rule of thumb, I want to see HHI that is at least three times the pro forma rent. As an example, let's say you have a place where the rents are $500 per month. If you multiply that by 12, you have $6,000 per year for rent. I then multiply that by the 3x rule of thumb I mentioned, giving me a total of $18,000. That means that a resident is going to need to have a household income of $18,000 or more to qualify to rent a $500 per month apartment.

Now, let's say the pro forma shows the units will be renovated and rents will be increased to $1,000 a month thereafter. Then I know the median HHI needs to be at least $36,000 to support that rent. If I look at the demographics and see that the submarket's HHI is only $25,000 a month, while that would be fine for rent of $500 a month rent, I'm going to have a problem trying to increase rents to $1,000 because the current resident base is not going to qualify to rent the apartments. They may be willing to sign a lease for $1,000, but that doesn't mean they will be able to pay for it, and then we have to deal with that.

Beyond the current employers and the population currently in the market, I also want to understand what could be coming in the future. Is there projected population growth? Is there any projected employment growth? What is that area doing (maybe giving incentives) to attract employers to come to the area? That's going to drive demand, which is what I am looking for. This will help bolster things such as rent growth. The higher the population, the more demand there is for housing. It's that simple. I want to be aware of new things that are being built in the area, especially if it's housing, because that could have an effect on the property. I also want to look at shopping and restaurants in the area plus any other amenities that make this a desirable place to live.

Determining value

Once I know that I like the market and the submarket, the next major item to be determined is the valuation of the property. Commercial real estate is valued through a simple mathematical formula. All investors use this to evaluate a property. This is the standard in the industry and is the way it is taught by everyone from online articles to podcasts to mentoring groups and even colleges.

When I moved to Boston, I thought about the fact that I never had a "formal" education in real estate and wanted to make sure I wasn't missing something. I went to classes at Boston University for a couple of years and obtained two certificates from their prestigious program: one in commercial real estate and the other in real estate finance. When I went to all those classes at BU, they taught it this way too.

This is *the* formula: **NOI** / Cap Rate = Value

> ### Backstage Glossary
>
> **NOI:** Net Operating Income. This is all of the property's income minus all of the expenses. The income includes not just rent but also items like pet rent, application fees, parking fees, any kind of income that's coming into the property. Expenses include items such as payroll, property insurance, utilities, maintenance, and repairs. NOI does not take into account any debt (mortgage) payments or items like depreciation and partnership expenses.

Here is why you needed to learn algebra in high school

In every area there will be a prevailing cap rate. This is the price where the deals in that market are trading versus their net operating income. By aggregating NOI and value from other completed deals within the defined market, you can then conclude a market's cap rate. It's simple algebra: you are just solving for cap rate now instead of value.

$$NOI / Cap\ Rate = Value$$

Becomes

$$Cap\ Rate = NOI / Value$$

Not every property is going to sell at the exact same cap rate, but when you review the market data, you will be able to determine the general range and average of where properties are trading. The cap rates may also vary depending on several factors, including the class of building.

Cap rates usually don't shift quickly; they move gradually over time. If the real estate market is in high demand, you will see cap rates go down because there's an inverse relationship between the cap rate and the value. If you plug some numbers in the valuation equation, you'll see that as a cap rate goes down, the valuation goes up. Conversely, in a market where there is less demand, the cap rates will go up.

I've gone into the technical detail of the valuation equation because it plays a pivotal role in deal analysis and is a frequent topic of discussion.

The next thing I look at when evaluating a deal for possible investment is that I want to understand the business plan. I want a property that has strong cash flow. Remember Keystone Concept #5: Cash Flow is King? You never lose money if you never have to sell. If I have a property with strong cash flow, I should be able to weather the storms of financial stress in the economy.

In general, real estate tends to appreciate over time. The values tend to go up, but there is no guarantee this will continue. I don't invest in properties and then just hope for market appreciation. This would mean investing in a property with a certain NOI and hoping that the cap rate goes down (because the market appreciated), thereby increasing the value of the property. There can be a number of reasons why a cap rate may go up or down, and these factors are beyond my control. Changes in the local area, government, the economy as a whole, investor demand, and interest rates all play a role in cap rates.

I like to invest in deals that offer the ability to "force appreciation." These are deals where we can make improvements to the property that I know will increase the value right away, rather than hoping that forces beyond my control turn out to be good for me. I invest in deals where I can affect changes at the property and increase the NOI myself.

These increases can be achieved by increasing income, lowering expenses, or both, which results in higher NOI. If the NOI is increased, then the value of the property is forced up—hence the term "forced appreciation." In the deals I invest in, we actually project that cap rates will go up (meaning the real estate market is softening), but the increase in NOI more than compensates for the change in cap rate. If cap rates don't go up as much, or at all, our profits are that much greater.

Do well by doing good

I've found the most effective way to force appreciation is by using a value-add strategy. This is a strategy in which we purchase an asset that is not at its best and highest use. It may be that this property was built 30 to 40 years ago and hasn't been updated since. Maybe the property hasn't been maintained well but there's an opportunity to add value by effecting even minor changes that make a big difference.

Often, value can be added by doing upgrades to the interiors by putting in new appliance packages, new paint, new flooring—things of that nature. There can also be an opportunity to fix the exterior of the property. Maybe it needs to be painted or the parking lots need to be redone or flower beds need to be planted. Perhaps we can add some amenities like a dog park.

Maybe there is a pool but it's dated and we can put in some new pool furniture, update a clubhouse, put in a fitness center—those types of amenities add up in terms of increased value, and they improve the quality of life for the folks who live there.

The interesting thing about the value-add strategy is that I had been implementing this strategy through all of my previous real estate deals. Starting with my very first primary residence in Manhattan, I made improvements to my unit and the building. I improved the land in Connecticut by building a house. I made some great upgrades to the building and unit on 76th Street. Finally, we made some really significant improvements to the property in Brooklyn, which had gone up in value quite a bit as a result. By instinct, I had already been utilizing this strategy for quite some time.

Here is an example of how a value-add strategy can pan out on an apartment complex. For this example, we will say we purchased a 100-unit apartment building and were able to implement improvements to the units that cost us $10,000 per unit. We spent one million dollars ($10K per unit x 100 units) on renovating this property. Due to these improvements, we are able to increase the rents by $100 per unit. Our rental income has increased by $10,000 per month, or $120,000 a year. If this property is in a market where the cap rate is 5%, just apply our valuation equation. $120,000 / .05 = $2,400,000. So, through this investment of $1 million, we have increased the property's cash flow by $120,000 per year, but even better, we have increased the value of the property by $2.4 million—a 140% return, more than doubling our $1 million investment!

With a value-add strategy we increase the NOI of the property, therefore increasing the value of the property. While we are holding that property, we receive cash flow in the form of distributions, but there is a large amount of profit that is produced upon sale. In a typical example, we are receiving a 10% return on our investment every year for a five-year holding period. At the end of those five years, we sell the property and receive 150% of our initial investment. So, on a sale like this, I would receive the full 100%

return of my initial investment in the deal plus an additional 50% profit. I also received a 50% return (10% per year) while holding the property, so I've doubled my investment in five years.

Using this approach has proven to be very effective in increasing my real estate portfolio over time. This isn't a get-rich-quick scheme. Some properties will perform better and some will underperform. But over time, I have found it to be very powerful in producing organic and sustainable growth that benefits everybody—me, my investors, and the people who live in our properties.

CHAPTER 8 LESSONS LEARNED

- By improving a property, you not only improve the lives of your residents, but you vastly increase your property values and do well by doing good.

- Learning basic algebra is a useful life skill when it comes to calculating deals and cap rates.

- It's important to do the math before investing, so you can size up your market in the present and calculate the future.

- Real estate is hyper-local, so beyond knowing your market, get to know your submarkets, sometimes even block by block.

- It's impossible to really know your goals until you can write them down.

- A plan is only as good as its execution. As you grow, check back with your plan monthly to chart your progress.

CHAPTER 9

SUNRISES IN KANSAS

With my passive investment plan well underway, it was time to focus my attention in the direction I knew that I really wanted to go—sponsoring my own deal. Based on my previous experience, and watching how sponsors were handling the deals I was investing in, I knew, or at least I was pretty sure, I would be good at it. I knew I had the skills to be successful, but would other people be comfortable investing a large amount of capital with me? Everyone has a first deal, and I believed that people would be willing to give me an opportunity. While my experience in real estate had been on a smaller scale, it had been quite successful. Plus, I had large scale parallel experience in a different industry.

For years, I had managed teams and budgets on multi-million-dollar projects in the advertising world. I managed large scale, global projects for Fortune 500 companies. I also had experience with overseeing and motivating teams to make sure things were getting done on time, on budget, and at the highest quality possible. I was certified by the Project Management Institute, which requires years of experience, courses, and a difficult exam. Most of these skills are directly transferable to managing the teams, budgets, and timelines as a sponsor in real estate. My project management experience, coupled with more than 10 years of part-time real estate projects, gave investors the confidence to invest with me for my first couple of deals, and then I started to build a track record.

But beyond having the skills for success, I was also driven by something larger. Remember the story about Benny from *Rent*? The original spark that got me involved in real estate? I had been guided from the beginning by the desire to reimagine the stereotype of the evil landlord and turn real estate investment into something that made life better for the people who lived in our properties.

While all of my deals are underwritten to make a substantial profit, I believe that the bottom line has to be about more than money. I am charting a different course for real estate investment as a form of activism by using my investment dollars, structuring my deals, and managing my properties in a way that makes my deals positive and productive for everybody.

Start with the ground you stand on, but don't get stuck in the mud

When I finally felt ready to step up and sponsor my first deal, I was living in South Florida and discovering that real estate prices there were comical. The first few times I heard the asking prices on the properties, I thought the listing agents were joking or trying to see if I was a fool who would pay these exorbitant prices. I was wrong—they were serious and had people snatching up properties at astronomical rates. Central Florida was a bit better, but it was still out of reach.

I spent the majority of the time I lived in Miami driving all over Florida, looking for a place to plunk down some money and do my first deal. I managed to find a few properties that worked well on paper and I submitted a letter of intent (**LOI**) for them.

> **Backstage Glossary**
>
> **LOI:** Letter of Intent. A non-legal document that is a written offer on the property. The document details major deal points to make sure the buyer and seller are in agreement. Having an LOI in place ensures that both parties are in agreement on the deal points before retaining lawyers to draft a sales agreement.

Learn how a deal moves and move with it

It's important to understand how the deal process is supposed to go down from start to finish, and what the normal procedure is, so you can be sure that any deal you are involved with moves according to accepted protocols. Here's a quick look at how things usually work.

1. The property is listed and the broker sends out an email about the property.

2. Interested parties request details on the property and begin their underwriting.

3. If the property looks good on paper, the buyer schedules a property tour with the broker. If they like the property, they can submit an offer via an LOI.

4. If the offer comes in at an acceptable price, it may be accepted. More often, however, the broker will set a "Call for Offers" date. The only way to get the property before that date would require your putting in a strong offer. In most cases, it's best for the seller to wait for the call for offers date and hope to get several parties bidding for the property. This can drive up the price.

5. All offers are due by the call for offers date. At that point, a broker will normally take all the offers, select the top group of them, and advance those to a best and final round.

6. During the best and final round, the broker often has a more extensive process where buyers submit their LOIs along with a questionnaire designed to help determine the buyer's strength and likelihood to close. The acquisition process can take a few months, so the broker wants to make sure the buyer will actually be able to close on the transaction and not waste everyone's time.

I submitted LOIs on a few properties in Florida and was advanced to best and final rounds, but I kept losing out. I was seeing properties sell for more than $1 million higher than my best and final offer.

Accept that life is complicated and that change can be your best friend

Of course, because nothing is ever simple, while all of this was going on, Erica was pregnant again. We had our second daughter that February in Miami. Nothing made me happier than seeing my almost three-year-old daughter holding our newborn in her arms.

The day our first daughter met her sister.

As fate would have it, and as these things often go in our lives, while Erica was out on maternity leave, she got an unexpected phone call from a colleague in New York. She was being recruited for a job up north, but to our surprise, it wasn't to go back to NYC. Instead, the offer was to run a theater in Boston. A move back to the northeast made a lot of sense to us. It was a tremendous opportunity for Erica to run a theater and to be in close connection and proximity to the NYC Broadway industry. Plus, to be honest, we weren't in love with Miami. The weather was great and we met fantastic people there, but it never really felt like home to us. Not the way New York did, anyway, or the way Boston would.

As for me, I had pretty much given up on real estate in Florida. I even did a brief spin around Ohio that hadn't turned up anything particularly hopeful. The deal flow there was slow, the properties weren't good, and I found that my potential investors didn't have the same twinkle in their eye when I mentioned Cleveland as when I would, say, Orlando. So, I decided to look somewhere else…how about Kansas City?

Many people ask me why I chose Kansas City. I raise some eyebrows when I drop that name because I think it seems a little random if you don't know the genesis of my interest there. The answer goes back to my acting days. One summer I was cast to do a couple of shows at Kansas City's Starlight Theater. This was one of my first union jobs, so the pay was somewhat decent (non-equity summer stock pay is a joke) but at that time, a decent wage was a huge step forward for me as an actor. I was very excited about the productions. We had a director with a good reputation, the leading roles were being played by people with Broadway credits, and I had a couple of nice supporting roles.

That gig felt like being welcomed into the royalty of repertory theatre in America. It was exciting. However, I was not at all excited about spending a summer in Kansas City. I was on the early side of my mid-20s and more than a little ignorant about the cultural geography of the Midwest. I imagined being in the middle of nowhere, stuck in a cornfield with no one to talk to but the cows. I had done a couple of summer stock seasons in the Midwest before, and that's what it had felt like. I was shocked when I arrived to find out the old showtune "Everything's Up to Date in Kansas City" was correct and I saw how metropolitan it really was. I had one of the most amazing summers of my life, and I've had a soft spot in my heart for Kansas City ever since.

Remember my friends Len and Tanisha? Well, they moved to Kansas City about the same time that we moved to Miami! This would be great; I could visit the city I liked so much and stay with my old friends. And this time, I could sleep in their guest room instead of crashing on their couch. Things were looking up for all of us NYC *Rent* crazy kids.

Good markets can be found in the darndest places

Erica and I decided to make the jump and move to Boston. I spent about three months before and another three months after our move on the phone with brokers and property managers in Kansas City, getting to meet them and taking a look at deals. At first glance, it seemed to me that some of these deals had numbers that were making a lot more sense to me than anything I'd seen in Florida. Once we were settled in Boston, I flew to KC for a week of meetings with brokers and property managers and started looking at properties in earnest.

I spent about a year looking at deals there with no luck. I was developing a severe case of senioritis, chomping at the bit to take the next step. But the next step just hadn't materialized, and I was getting impatient. Despite struggling to find a deal, I clicked with one property management company. The company had been around since the 1980s and had a wide range of experience in the local markets. Several brokers had recommended them, especially for a value-add strategy, which is what I was looking to do. I had reviewed different deals with them as I was analyzing opportunities from brokers.

One day, I was on the phone with my contact, a regional manager. We were reviewing a deal that I was considering. Unfortunately, it did not meet my criteria. I think she could hear the disappointment in my voice and mentioned to me quietly that she had a client in Lawrence, Kansas, with two sister properties, 132 units in total, that her team managed. I learned that the owners were about to put the property on the market and she thought it was exactly what I was looking for. She offered to put me in touch with the broker who was going to be listing the property.

I started to do research on Lawrence and I liked what I saw. Lawrence, Kansas, is a small college town about a 40-minute drive west of Kansas City and 30 minutes east from Topeka, the state capital. While Lawrence is its own MSA, it's not that far from major cities and a lot of the deals done in that area are handled by brokers based in Kansas City. The town is home to the University of Kansas (Rock Chalk, Jayhawk!), has a population of around 100,000 and is named in the top 10 in several publications for attributes such as launching a business and work-life balance. It's also known as one of the most centrally located cities in the United States—it's smack dab in the middle of America.

Lawrence was home to the "Free-State" movement and has a local brewery named Free State (with some very tasty adult beverages). During the "Bleeding Kansas" period of the 1850s, "Free-Stater" was the name given to settlers in Kansas who opposed the expansion of slavery. The name derives from the term "free state," that is, a U.S. state without slavery. Many of the Free-Staters joined the Jayhawkers in their fight against slavery.

Lawrence was founded by the New England Emigrant Aid Company (NE-EAC), a Boston-based transportation company, and was named for Amos Adams Lawrence, a Republican abolitionist originally from Massachusetts who offered financial aid and support for the settlement. The main street in the town is called Massachusetts Street. Seriously? If this wasn't a sign that this was the town for me, I didn't know what was!

The properties in Lawrence were called Sunrise Place and Sunrise Village and were within two miles of each other. I did several rounds of in-depth underwriting on the portfolio and reviewed it with the property manager. Since the management company was already managing the property, they needed to keep a little bit of distance from the sale because there could be a conflict of interest. They were able to speak with me in generalities. They would be managing the property after purchase. I liked them, and they had been managing the property for a couple of years, so this would be a seamless transition. The broker told me the seller was expecting $12M for the property. My underwriting had me at $9.5M. So, I called my friend Justin.

You may be wondering, who is Justin? Well, let me tell you, Justin was a very important development in my story.

Good things come to those who wait, persist, and follow through

I met Justin through a mentorship group I had joined. He'd been in the group for a while and had a vast amount of experience in the multifamily world. But what drew me to him was his background. His dad was in the concession foods business just like my dad, so we had a lot in common. Both of us had worked for our dads and both of us knew how to sell a hot dog at a county fair, it was BFF territory at first sight.

KEYSTONE CONCEPT #15
Choose Partners Who Know More Than You Do
Partner up with people who are more experienced than you. You may be able to bring something to the table that compliments their skills and they will bring enormous value because of their greater experience and knowledge. Then, as you grow, reach up and down to help newer investors.

Justin was a "coach" in the mentorship program. I asked him if he wouldn't mind looking at a deal I was reviewing, and things grew organically from there.

Justin and I looked at the Lawrence deal. We were able to make some minor tweaks here and there, and managed to push the purchase price up to $10 million but that was the ceiling. I had to get the price of the property under that number. I reached out to the broker again and let her know that I was quite far from the $12 million price she mentioned. She told me I should put my offer in. I asked if she was sure and explained that I didn't want to insult anyone by coming in too low. She reassured me that she didn't think anyone would be offended.

While she never came out and said it, I had a feeling that maybe she thought the $12 million was high and that offers would likely come in lower and that I should give it a shot. I didn't want to come in at the full $10 million. It felt like there was going to be another round, and I wanted to leave myself some wiggle room. I discussed the deal with Justin and I asked him if he wanted to partner with me on the deal. He said he was interested, so I continued to lead the negotiations but kept him informed throughout the process.

Make your offer and wait

I initially offered $9.3 million for the property. I felt like this was a good first offer so I could see how things stood before I showed my full hand. My offer went in the day before the call for offers. I spoke with the broker that day to make sure she received it and I reviewed the offer with her verbally to make sure everything was clear. She thanked me and then there was nothing to do but wait, which is sometimes the hardest part of negotiating a deal.

It took a couple of long weeks to receive feedback. The suspense was killing me. When I finally spoke with the broker, she explained there were multiple owners and it that it takes a while to get them all together and on the same page. Bottom line—my offer came in right around the same range as all the others. Since all of the offers were so much lower than the asking price, the owners decided they were not going to sell the property and pulled it from the market.

My heart sank!

All that time and effort (again!) on a deal that looked like it might work out. I was so disappointed. I had analyzed over 100 properties at that point (117 to be exact). I'd gotten good at underwriting but still had no deals and was beyond frustrated. How could this happen? I was determined not to let this go. I was not going to take "no" for an answer.

I called the broker and spoke with her. We'd had a few conversations during this process and I found her likable and approachable. I felt that a candid conversation with her would be helpful, so I could figure out where I was going wrong and what I could do differently. What was I missing?

It turned out—I hadn't done anything wrong. The broker said she felt I did everything right. My underwriting was on point. That's why the other offers that came in were in the same range as mine. She explained to me that the owners had the same view that I did. They felt that if they began to implement a value-add on the property within the next six months they would be able to prove out that model, increase their NOI and then be able to sell at the higher valuation. I thought they were right, but that was what *I* wanted to do. If they did that, there really wouldn't be any profit left on the table for me and my investors. My perfect deal was about to go up in smoke.

So, I spoke with the broker about this. I was essentially trying to sell her on why it made sense for them to sell the property. I gave her information to relay to the sellers to convince them that even though it would be a lower price than they'd anticipated, they should sell the property to me. I shared my underwriting with her and had many more in-depth conversations about the property and the market itself. Interest Rates were on their way up, did the owners really want to take on the risk of cap rates going up as well? She would talk to the owners, get their feedback, and come back to me. This went on and on for a few weeks until finally I signed a contract to buy the property for $9.9 million!

Pop the champagne corks! Well, not quite yet...but we were getting there. I was beyond thrilled to have my first deal under contract, but had no idea what was in store for me over the next couple of months as I began the acquisition processes. This is when I realized that mentorship programs are a lot like big screen romances. It's all about the courtship and eventually the wedding. Nobody tells you that the real work begins once you get married, and there is no three-ring binder to tell you how to do that.

I knew all about acquiring a property, underwriting a property, and getting an offer accepted. And that was where my knowledge ended, leaving me in midair after jumping headfirst off the diving board. This is why I was glad I had Justin as my co-sponsor on the deal. He had been in the water and in the deep end a few times before. It was good to have someone to turn to when the waves kicked up, which they inevitably did.

Gather a group of investors who see things like you do

Now that we had a deal under contract, I needed investors. That meant I needed sales tools. I reached out to a graphic designer I knew from my ad agency days and had him put together a PowerPoint template that showed all the information on the sponsors, the market, and the deal, including all the financial underwriting for those who really wanted to understand the mechanics of the deal. When it was all laid out, it looked like the great deal that it was. It was investor advantaged, I was taking no fees, very little equity, and I was promising my investors a 15.30% **IRR** (Internal Rate of Return).

Backstage Glossary

IRR: The Internal Rate of Return, an important metric for investors when evaluating the performance of an investment. IRR measures the return of an investment over time. The exact same return, over a shorter period of time, will result in a higher IRR because you get your money faster. It's important to understand how an IRR functions because it measures the profitability of a deal by including how long it will take to realize this return.

We scheduled a live online webinar and invited everyone to join as Justin and I walked through the details of the offering, followed by a Q&A period at the end. I recorded the whole thing and later sent it to anyone who was unable to join us live.

I had heard stories about sponsors who get their deals fully funded within a couple of days of their release. Ours took a bit longer, about four weeks. I was honestly sweating after two weeks when we were only half funded, but the rest came in. After week four, when we were full, more investors were saying they wanted to subscribe. I wanted to say—where were you two weeks ago when I was freaking out? Instead, I politely informed them the project was fully funded but that I would be happy to let them know about future opportunities.

Be willing to wait to lock in the rate

As we approached the closing date, I wanted to lock in the loan at a low interest rate. This is something I had been keeping an eye on throughout the entire purchase process, which had taken about 75 days. As our bad luck would have it, interest rates were slowly creeping up. We had underwritten conservatively at 5.15% even though the rates were below 5% when we started this process. But they kept creeping up and I was getting worried. I reached out to the lender repeatedly, wanting to lock in the rate but, inevitably, they needed another piece of information. And then another, and another. All I could do was wait, because after all, you can't push a river. Finally, a few days before we were scheduled to close, I was told we could lock the interest rate at 5.1%.

Our loan term

Our business plan for Sunrise Properties was to hold the property for approximately five years. However, we went with a loan with a 12-year term, 30-year amortization. We made this choice because no one can reliably predict where the market will be in five years. We didn't want to be in a position, if the real estate market was soft, of selling the property because our finance term was ending. In a down market, having an additional seven years on the loan term would give us plenty of time to hold our cash-flowing property and wait for market conditions to improve.

Of course, prepayment of a loan comes with a penalty. A prepayment penalty is a fee for paying off a mortgage before the term is over. Lenders like to have the steady stream of profit they receive from a mortgage, and they don't want them paid off early. Most large mortgages, therefore, have some sort of penalty if you pay in full more than a few months before the maturity (the end of the term) of the loan.

Prepayment penalties

There are three very common types of prepayment penalties: step-down, yield maintenance, and defeasance. With step-down, there is a stated percentage fee based on the mortgage, which is gradually reduced over time. A typical step-down penalty for a 10-year mortgage is based on a percentage of the loan balance and would look like 5% for the first and second year of the mortgage, 4% for years three and four, 3% for years five and six, 2% for years seven and eight, and 1% for the final two years.

A yield maintenance penalty protects the lender, making sure they will be able to receive the same profit they would if the property was held for the full term of the loan. They look at the profit based on the current interest rate vs the interest rate of the loan. If rates have gone up and the lender can make the same or more profit by deploying that capital into another investment, the penalty will be low, but they usually make the penalty a minimum of 1% of the unpaid balance. But if rates have gone down, the penalty will be the difference between what they would have made from the loan vs what they can get now.

Defeasance is similar to yield maintenance in that it protects the lender's returns. However, the mechanism by which that is accomplished is complicated, involving securities intermediaries and other consultants. The borrower purchases a portfolio of government bonds and transfers them to a special-purpose entity called a successor borrower. The effect is the same as yield maintenance; the original owner of the property is released from its financial obligations.

When we got our loan, interest rates were on their way up. The Federal Reserve had made several statements that they were expecting to raise the rates for the remainder of the year and continue that trend in the following year. Therefore, locking in at the current interest rate seemed like a good idea. We discussed a step-down penalty as an option with our lender and were informed that we would pay a higher interest rate if we wanted that.

One last consideration for us was that we were getting a Fannie Mae loan. This loan was assumable, meaning that someone could take over our loan if we wanted to sell it. This would avoid the prepayment penalty. There would be an assumption charge of 1%, but if the rates at our time of sale were such that the prepayment penalty was very high, an assumption could be an option. The other nice feature of the loan was that it had a supplemental available. This allows the borrower to take out an additional mortgage on the property (if the property's financials support it). This way, an owner could take some equity out of the property, like a traditional re-finance, without having to actually refinance the property and trigger the prepayment penalty.

Based on all these factors, the best option at the time seemed to be to go with the Fannie Mae loan with the yield maintenance penalty. Once the rate was locked, we were pretty much set to close, we just needed the final loan documents signed.

I know it's boring and makes you squint, but always read the fine print

So, here is the weird thing when you're doing a deal. When you are finally closing on the property, all they send you are the signature pages for the loan documents. You sign two copies of these pages in blue ink and then mail them to the bank's attorney or the title company, and that's that. They don't send you the actual agreement documents. All you see are those signature pages, so you have no idea what you actually just signed. That sounds crazy, right? But that's how things are done. That's the way it's been for me and I've done quite a few transactions with different lenders etc. Always the same deal. Signature pages. The end.

The first time I came across this was when I was a **Key Principal** (KP) / **Guarantor** on someone else's deal. I received an email telling me to print the attached signature pages, sign them and FedEx them to an attorney. I told them, "No way." They told me I was holding up the closing, and they really applied the pressure, but I told them, "I don't care." I wasn't signing signature pages for a document I'd never seen. I was told that the documents wouldn't be ready until the next day, so I should send the signature pages now and then I'd read what I signed after the fact. I told them quite simply, "No."

Backstage Glossary

Key Principal: A term used by agency lenders (Fannie Mae and Freddie Mac). Often abbreviated as "KP" this person controls or manages a deal, is critical to its success, and may sign as a guarantor on a loan.

Backstage Glossary ─────────────

Guarantor: a Key Principal or other person who signs an agreement guaranteeing the payment of the loan.

You should know you can slow the process down. You can say, "no." The world won't end (most of the time, anyway), and if the deal dies because of a brief delay, you shouldn't have been in the deal in the first place.

They were really exasperated with me and explained that since this was a Fannie Mae deal, the language is boiler plate and can't even be changed if there is something in it that I don't like. I told them I wanted to read it first, regardless. I also asked, "If it's boiler plate, why can't you send it to me?" They said they hadn't filled in the blanks yet, that would be done the next day. I said, "Well, send me the blank boiler plate so I can read it without the blanks filled in and get comfortable with the wording." They sent it the next morning, I read it that day and sent off signed docs that afternoon.

Much ado about nothing, but you have to read everything you sign. It's a rule I've never regretted following.

On all my deals, I make sure my attorney knows *explicitly* that I need to review the documents a few days prior to closing. I keep on top of this. Apparently, a lot of people in this business don't read the documents when they are signing on loans worth tens or even hundreds of millions of dollars. I am not one of those people. I read the fine print because I know the devil is always in the details and the people who are pressuring you to sign aren't the ones who are going to be responsible for the debt. That responsible person would be you.

> ## KEYSTONE CONCEPT #16
> ### Luke, Trust Your Feelings
>
> If your gut is telling you something is wrong, listen to yourself. Pull back on the reins until you feel comfortable. You don't have to do anything. Channel your inner Obi-Wan Kenobi and make sure you feel good about everything going on with a deal and don't be afraid to push back or even walk away from the table. If something feels amiss, there is probably a reason.

Success is a long and winding road

I remember my first property purchases in New York and Connecticut. I would go to an office with a conference room. There would be all sorts of people there: buyer, seller, attorneys, bank attorneys, title agents, property managers, etc. I would sit down for an hour or so and sign all types of documents and at the end be given a set of keys. A celebration would take place. Everyone would shake hands, congratulating one another with much fanfare, and the transaction would be closed.

When closing day arrived for my first big multifamily acquisition—I'd sealed the deal on 132 units for $10 million dollars after working toward this for two years, traveling countless miles, and spending thousands of hours—was there a cake and a marching band and bottles of champagne popping? No, there was not. It wasn't even in an office. Signature pages were sent via FedEx and the next day there was a two-sentence email from the title agent informing me that we had closed and that the deed had been recorded.

That was an emotional moment for me. In fact, I fell into my chair and shed a few tears. The whole thing was such an emotional ride. I'd poured so much of myself into it. I was stressed out, and now I could finally relax. I was having a moment of release and relief. And of course, extreme pride. I was proud of myself for scaling what had seemed like an impossible mountain. I don't think I have ever worked so hard for something in my entire life, and that's saying something. To have finally achieved this was a bit overwhelming.

Erica walked into the room. She looked at me and was puzzled. "Are you crying?" she asked.

"Oh, shut up," I said, and gave her a big hug.

A few minutes later, when I had composed myself, I sent an email to all the investors to let them know we'd closed. I posted the news on Facebook—my friends went berserk. It was a special moment. And while it wasn't popping champagne, Erica did bring me a Basil Hayden on the rocks (my personal favorite) at dinner that night.

Putting a win-win deal into action

Now that I owned the property, the real work could begin! The property transition was smooth because we retained the property management company that had been managing the property for years. The staff stayed the same, so for them and the residents at the property it was almost as if nothing happened. Except for one big change—we were going to improve the property.

The previous ownership had done everything they could to keep expenses as low as possible, and the place was in pretty bad shape as a result. The buildings themselves were in poor condition, and many systems were in need of repair or maintenance. The sidewalks around the property had been worn down to rubble. We decided this was the first item we would tackle.

I was first introduced to Pavement Pete during due diligence. Pete pulled up in his beat-up pickup truck, got out huffing and puffing and walked toward me. At first glance, Pete looked like hell: rumpled, overstuffed, out of breath, and over confident. All kinds of red flags were raised as he got closer. Pete, I was soon to learn, was a good ol' Kansas boy sent to bid on the sidewalks. He told me he'd been doing business in town for many years and that he poured the original concrete when the properties were built in the 1980s. He was like the mayor of pavement.

A couple of weeks after closing, I was onsite with Pete. He had a few cans of spray paint and we walked both properties and marked the areas to be repaired and replaced and discussed in detail what he would be doing at each place. I was accompanied by our head maintenance tech and the property manager. Then we gave him the green light to start and things went well for about a week or two.

That year Kansas got hit by a lot of snow and ice early in the fall, and things went downhill quickly. Pete and his team took forever to make progress on the property. While the weather was not his friend, it could hardly explain the lengthy delays. Then, after all the waiting, they did an incredibly sloppy job. The workmanship was subpar. We were spending tens of thousands of dollars on concrete and it looked terrible. They damaged the property with "overspray," which means that the concrete wound up on doors and siding and even the lawns. It was a truly sloppy job.

I was upset with Pavement Pete and with the management company, who recommended him. They had been wonderful up to this point. They said they didn't understand why I was upset with them—after all, it was my choice to use Pavement Pete, he wasn't someone that they had recommended. WHAT? They were the ones who brought in Pete. That's why I made the decision to go with him.

The situation became very confusing, but we eventually sorted out what had happened. Pete had been recommended by the seller, who'd had the work quoted shortly before listing the property for sale and Pete's was the lowest bid. The property management company had to stay impartial since they were still working for the seller when I was introduced to him during due diligence. They didn't say they recommended Pete, but I assumed they did since they had set up my initial meeting with him.

Lesson learned on being extra careful about such things when a previous owner's property manager is going to be the one you hire as well.

Luckily, we were able to catch up with Pete before too much damage was done. We'd planned on repainting all the doors anyway since they were mismatched blues, greens, and whites, which looked horrible when you pulled up to the property. We got Pete to come back and fix some of the sloppy work and repair some of the damage. We considered filing a suit against him, but ultimately it didn't seem worth the time and legal expense. We cut ties and had another contractor come in and finish the job. The new contractor was much more expensive but did a stellar job in a timely fashion. Just another reminder of a thing I've learned before: "You get what you pay for."

Green is about more than money

Next up were our green program improvements. We had gotten a lower interest rate on our loan by agreeing to make environmental improvements to the property. This program was an offering from Fannie Mae and they sent an engineer to the property during the acquisition process to determine what improvements would be needed to reduce water consumption at the property by 25%.

We replaced over 300 toilets along with shower heads and bathroom and kitchen sink aerators. Our residents were thrilled when the work was complete, which took about two weeks. Their units had been improved and they saw their water bills cut by more than a quarter. We were also doing a positive thing for the planet—which made us feel good.

From a property owner's perspective, we didn't see a change on the utilities since the water was individually metered and charged directly to the residents. But we did receive the benefits of the reduced interest rate on our loan and having happy residents. With these and the other improvements we were making around the properties, the residents loved us, which never hurts.

Our plan was to make improvements to the property's common areas first, and then, as people moved out as they naturally do, we would renovate the individual units. That would allow us to raise the rent; we were well below market rate when we took over because the place was such a mess.

Our business plan assumed a typical amount of attrition at the property and that those units would be renovated and then rented at a corresponding $200 increase. The issue that we ended up facing was that very few people wanted to leave. We increased rent $100 per unit on a renewal, but it was still the best deal in town, particularly since we were now owners who cared about the property, which is an added bonus for residents.

Owners who are attentive to residents' requests, who are making repairs and improving their community are hard to come by in middle-income properties. So, we were achieving $100 increases on rents instead of the $200 we had planned on, and this put an obvious dent in our business plan. Sure, we were weren't spending money on interior improvements, but those funds were earmarked for that expense only and were held in an escrow account with our lender until the work was performed. Therein lies the rub.

This situation caused our cash flow to be lower than we had projected for our first year of operations. The property was doing well otherwise, and we started distributions of cash to our investors earlier than expected, just three months after acquisition. Although distributions weren't quite at the level we had projected; we explained why this was happening to the investors and they understood.

Our NOI was increasing but cash flow was just a bit under, due to the lack of turnover, and we still had that pile of cash sitting in the bank. As we progressed into our second year of operations, we increased rents again to keep pace with the market. For our renewals, we still were well under market, but we started to see some movement and were able to quickly renovate and lease out the improved units now for an increase of $225 on the four-bedroom units.

One of things I learned from this property was how hard it is to find good maintenance personnel. We had kept the original maintenance team when we acquired the property and we went through many permutations of that team. We gave raises and offered incentives and treated them well, but we still went through six team members until we hit on the right combination. When we did, it was worth the wait. I've since experienced this same challenge to a lesser extent with almost all my other properties. I've spoken with other owners about it too; it seems to be ubiquitous in the industry.

In real estate, just as in poker, you've got to "know when to hold 'em, know when to fold 'em, know when to walk away, know when to run"

Things were moving along well at Sunrise Properties. The real estate market remained hot. We'd owned the property for about a year when brokers first started calling. They were interested in seeing how the property was performing and if we would be interested in selling. By the time we hit the 16-month mark in December of 2019 our NOI was looking strong and cap rates in Lawrence had compressed a bit with some recent sales. We decided to start to speak with the brokers about the valuation of the portfolio.

The properties looked great and were performing well. We had done all the heavy lifting, completed all the exterior work, and were upgrading interiors gradually. We had a proven model and it was working. A new owner could come in and continue to renovate the interiors as we were doing, and they would have a very profitable venture. Our NOI was in the mid $60,000 range per month and climbing quickly. At $65,000 per month, $780,000 per year, at a 6 cap (where we bought it, but cap rates were compressing), this would be a $13 million valuation. We would need to sell at about $13.5 million to double our investors' money. With our NOI climbing, we knew we would be at that valuation by March. We could sell the property in less than two years and double investors' money—a home run!—and on my first time at bat.

There was just one issue. That pesky prepayment penalty. Now you understand why I went into great detail a little earlier in this chapter to explain the mechanics of that. Remember, we had gone with a yield maintenance penalty. When we closed on the property, it was our best choice, given the data we had at that time. Interest rates were on their way up in mid-2018. The Federal Reserve said it was planning to continue the hikes for the remainder of 2018 and at least two more hikes in 2019.

Life happens, so learn to adjust your expectations, and your game plan

By the end of 2018 I was seeing interest rates in the 5.25% to 5.50% range. We had locked in at 5.10% and felt like we had a great deal. But then in 2019, rates came down. Way down. By the end of that year, we were looking at rates in the upper 3% to low 4% range. If we were to sell the property, we would now have a huge prepayment penalty that would erase all of our profit on the deal.

The good news was that we had an assumable loan. This meant a buyer could purchase the property from us and take over our debt and then we would just be subject to a 1% assumption fee, which wasn't bad. If we could find someone who wanted our property and didn't mind paying the higher interest rate, we would be able to sell and get out clean. Of course, the buyer who would be assuming our debt at an interest rate considerably above the current rates would want a discount on the sales price. But how much of a discount?

We were in discussions with a broker who had just sold another complex in Lawrence across the street from one of the properties. Based on that recent sale, the broker felt confident he could find a buyer for us who would assume the debt and offer a strong price. In late February of 2020, we decided we would go to market and see where the offers came in.

The broker started putting together the marketing package in March and then, guess what happened? The entire world was put into a tailspin by the global coronavirus pandemic. So that put things on hold for a few months.

A word about Covid

Saying that dealing with the COVID-19 pandemic was challenging for everybody would be an understatement. But I'm proud of the way we were able to face those challenges responsibly and push through them.

In response to the pandemic, we implemented the following measures to ensure the safety and well-being of everyone connected to our businesses: staff, residents, and the surrounding communities.

- We put a moratorium on evictions because we wanted all of our residents to feel safe and secure during those difficult times.

- We helped guide residents to local and federal resources where they could access financial help.

- We deferred any non-emergency maintenance and moved to virtual tours to reduce in-person contact and keep our staff and residents safe.

- We reduced or removed all non-essential expenses to stay lean and agile through the crisis.

- We increased our charitable giving to organizations that really needed it that year including the CDC Foundation, Broadway Cares, and Caritas Communities.

By the end of May, it seemed like everyone was starting to get their footing and adapt to the "new abnormal" of life during what was clearly going to be an extended struggle with the virus. The good news was that the property was still performing very well despite the pandemic.

We put the property on the market and we set a call for offers date in early July. The offers came in, but due to the loan assumption requirements, there weren't as many and they weren't as high as we had hoped. The U.S. Treasury had dropped a total of 2.4% since we had locked the rate in 2018, which made our prepayment penalty nearly $3.5M. The thought of the home run had been an appealing one, but now it was looking like the best we could hope for was a standup double. This was still pretty good, but I had set the bar high and it felt disappointing compared to my grand slam dreams.

I decided to create a brand-new pro forma analysis on the property. Given that we had been operating the property for a year and a half at this point, I had a firm grasp on how it operated, and what the expenses were. I re-forecasted the next three years based on all of that information but also factoring in COVID-19. Our initial model had yearly rent increases, but as we were at the beginning of the pandemic and didn't know if it would last a year or two (or more?) that possibility seemed remote.

The U.S. economy suffered a titanic 33% plunge in the second quarter of 2020, and all data pointed to a drawn-out recovery. I created a new pro forma, keeping our rents flat, with no growth for the next two years. This model showed that we would get less cash-on-cash during the hold period, but we might still be able to achieve our projected IRR. However, the offers that came in had us selling the property now, removing any further risk (such as coronavirus and recession) and walking away with an IRR that beat our projections by a large margin.

Be transparent with your investors and give them a voice in the discussion

My partner Justin and I were pretty sure we wanted to sell but we wanted to give our investors a chance to weigh in. We sent out a survey and had a company meeting online where we went through all the scenarios that were available to us. The response from the investors was incredible. They all wanted us to sell the property and, more than that, they were thrilled with the strong return on investment that we would be bringing them. All of this was in the middle of a pandemic when people needed cash the most.

Unlike the acquisition process, there wasn't too much to do on the sale. We needed to provide all our business documents and allow for inspections. And then—just like the purchase, with no fanfare or trumpet flourishes—we closed. But this time, I had a wire transfer of several millions of dollars to show for my efforts. The next day, I was beaming with pride as I wired that money to the 40 investors who had come along with me for a fun, uplifting, and profitable ride, even during a pandemic!

CHAPTER 9 LESSONS LEARNED

- When you are sponsoring a deal, make sure your investors are as fully informed as you would want to be.

- Change is the only constant in life, and in real estate. So, remain agile. Be able to adjust your expectations and your game plan to keep pace with the facts.

- There is more to success than just the bottom line.

- Savor your successes, moments like that don't come along every day. Taking the opportunity to celebrate your wins goes a long way toward carrying you through the tougher moments down the line.

- I know it's hard, and definitely boring, but read the fine print. Know what you are signing before you sign it no matter what anybody says or how much pressure you are under to hurry and close.

- Sometimes a hard "no" from a seller just means finding a different road to solving their problem and getting to "yes!"

CHAPTER 10

BUYING A MULTIFAMILY
OUT OF THIN AIR

Through some creative use of advanced real estate strategies, I sold this....

And I bought this:

How, you might ask, was it possible for me to purchase a multi-family property literally out of thin air? Pretty nifty trick, right? Well, it's not that simple and it's going to take me two chapters to explain how I pulled this off. So, grab a cup of coffee and take some notes, there will be a quiz later.

At this time, we had moved to Boston, but do you remember the townhome in Brooklyn— the accidental house hack that we talked about in Chapter 5? It was a two-unit property that we'd bought; we lived in one unit and rented the other. When we moved to Miami, we rented out both units, and the property more than paid for itself. It had been cash flow positive ever since, so we hung on to it.

You may also remember that next door to the property was an eyesore—a large ex-Kentucky Fried Chicken with an enormous vacant parking lot that had been abandoned years before. I saw this blight on the neighborhood as a huge opportunity because I knew that, given the cost of properties in the area, it was extremely unlikely that another fast-food restaurant would open there. The economics didn't support it. I suspected that eventually someone would purchase the property, build some nice condos, and our property value would rise. I had also thought that maybe, just maybe, if we got really lucky, that condo developer would want to buy the "air rights" our property was already zoned for, which I'll explain in more detail in just a moment.

From the time that we bought our property, I would frequently check the city's Department of Finance and Department of Buildings websites in search of a sale or building permits for that lot. About four years went by with nothing happening. Then, as my good luck would have it, one day out of the clear blue sky, I got a phone call. The woman on the other end of the line was a representative for a company and she informed me that they had just purchased the lot. She said she was calling to be neighborly and introduce herself.

I thought that was very neighborly of her indeed, and so we had a nice chat. She told me they had acquired nearly the entire block and were working on the final parcel. They wanted to be good neighbors, and obviously there would be construction going on in the future. We would chat about that when the time came, but for now, she just wanted to reach out and introduce herself.

That night, I excitedly explained to Erica that someone had bought the lot. We were thrilled, mainly because of the mosquitos! I didn't tell you about the mosquitos yet? Well, hold on, and allow me to digress for a moment. When we moved into that house in March of 2014, one of the first items on our agenda was to fix up the miserable backyard.

I'm not a gardener, but clearly something had to be done. I spent hours driving to and from Home Depot and a landscaping shop, gathering equipment and supplies. We removed the chain link fence and replaced it with an attractive wood fence. I took out the dilapidated gardening shed, leveled the ground, and uncovered all sort of things like chicken bones (courtesy of the old KFC next door) and even a set of false teeth—I know, gross. Once that was done, I laid down new soil and then sod. A border of river rocks framed the yard as a final touch. In the end, we had a beautiful backyard.

Backyard: Before

Backyard: After

Then, just as the weather was starting to get nice and warm and we were ready to enjoy our brand-new back yard, they showed up. The mosquitos, swarms of them, and not just at night, but all the time. They were a special breed that feeds at all hours. Day in and day out, night in and night out, those voracious flying beasts took over until we couldn't even enjoy our yard. I bought a contraption called "the mosquito magnet" from an online store. It did a good job luring and capturing mosquitos, and I knew it was working because each time I emptied it, there were gazillions of little mosquito corpses. But not even the mosquito magnet was enough to cull the teeming population of pests.

It was clear to me that these tiny savages were breeding next door in the standing water around the abandoned KFC. And they weren't just in the backyard anymore. They were fanning out along the perimeter. There was always an attack squadron of them waiting by our front door. The entrance to our unit was underneath the steps to the upper unit, so it was a cozy, shaded, and somewhat confined place, perfect for them to hover, waiting for us. We had to run as fast as possible to get into our home. I think I set world records for speed, unlocking our doors. I even reached out to our city council member to try to resolve this issue, but it didn't help.

Once we moved to Miami, the mosquitos didn't interfere with our daily lives anymore. Our tenants, however, complained loudly, and I didn't blame them one bit. We actually built out the area under the stairs into an enclosed vestibule which eliminated the mosquitoes' ability to ambush unsuspecting humans by the front entrance, but they were still in the backyard, and we warned new tenants about them before they signed a lease.

Needless to say, when we learned from my nice new neighbor that the mosquito breeding factory would be brought down, we were relieved. This would also be a great thing for our property value. The removal of this eyesore would be a huge improvement.

And then came the issue of our air rights. We knew we had extra "air rights" that we could potentially sell to anyone buying the lot next door. I had done some research on this when we purchased the property to understand what this was and how it worked, so that I would be educated in case an opportunity to sell the rights arrived; it turned out to be quite an extensive education. Here's a brief primer on air rights.

Air rights 101

Air rights involve a unique set of rules that differ from city to city. Since this took place in NYC, I will discuss how air rights work there. New York has zoning laws that every property must follow. The individual rules for each zone, and information about which zone each lot is located in, can be found through the city's ZoLa (Zoning and Land Use) website.

The amount of developable square footage on any lot is calculated using a metric called the "floor area ratio" (**FAR**). If you haven't used up all the FAR on a property, you have the right to develop on your property until all the FAR is utilized, as long as you follow the other zoning rules. These development rights (aka air rights) can also be transferred to a neighboring property. If you do this, you are selling them your rights to build additional square footage. You no longer can build that additional square footage, but you still keep your property.

Backstage Glossary

FAR: Floor Area Ratio determines how much square footage a building can have as a ratio of the square footage of the land it sits on. The smaller the building's footprint in relation to the land it sits on, the higher you can build.

The FAR on a property is based on the zoning. Our property was in the R7B zone, which has a 3.0 FAR. This meant we had three times the amount of square footage of the lot as usable floor area. Our lot measured 1,675 square feet, so this meant we could legally have 5,025 square feet of usable space. However, the building was only 3,158 square feet, leaving us with 1,867 square feet of developable space. We could build another floor or two on top of our existing property if we wanted to (to a maximum of 1,867 square feet), as long as we followed the height, setback, and other requirements as defined in the zoning code.

We actually looked into this with an architect not too long after we moved into the property, but we decided the additional revenue generated by doing this was not worth the additional cost. Now, we had someone buying the lot next door and we wanted to sell these additional rights to them. I didn't want to seem too eager, so I didn't bring it up on the first phone conversation. I wanted to see if they would bring it up. I was playing the long game.

Doing your homework can really pay off

At this point, I moved into major research mode—scouring the Internet for information on the prices people were paying for air rights. I also wanted to understand the technicalities of how all of this worked. I had heard from someone that selling your air rights meant that the building next door could cantilever their building so it would actually come over the property line and go up above my building. This turned out to be an urban legend. They can't do that without express permission.

As was becoming my ritual before any decision, I turned to my trusted team of advisors, my community of trust, to get their thoughts and guidance. In this case, I looked to my friend Jon, whose family owned a lot of property in the city, and I also reached out to a Brooklyn developer I had become friendly with. I spoke with them about the situation and tried to get an idea of how to value air rights. Once I had a price, I patiently waited a few months to see if our new neighbor-developers would inquire about purchasing them. Week after week went by, and they didn't even mention air rights when we spoke from time to time.

They did reach out about an access agreement so they could access my property, mainly to protect my property as they built their new building.

Still, no discussion of the air rights came up and I started to feel like their plans were getting to the point of no return. I might lose my chance to have a discussion about the possibility. So, one day while I was on the phone with the nice woman from the developer's office, I told her that I had development rights available on the property and that I'd be happy to discuss this with them if there was any interest. They might have been playing me, but it seemed like I did this just in time. She said that they were just finalizing the plans with the architect and it might be too far along but she would check with the team.

What have I done? I thought to myself, trying not to let my anxiety register in my voice. Did I hold out too long and blow my chance to sell the rights? Fortunately, the developer said she would take another look at everything. She ran her calculations and saw that it would make sense for them to purchase our air rights! We negotiated a price and came to an agreement and went forward with the sale.

Then, as I was doing all my research and homework, I looked at my survey and noticed that a few feet of my property also fell within another zone. This zone had a greater FAR, so I actually had 2,597 square feet of space that I was allowed to sell. Now, I was a novice at this but this is what it looked like to me. If I was right and this was accurate, it meant I had 40% more development rights then I originally thought. It was incredible to have this extra value fall in our lap due to the research I had conducted.

We went through the process of putting all of the legal paperwork together. I had the developer cover my legal expenses and I hired a zoning attorney. We drafted the property agreements and included that I would have an engineering firm oversee everything on our end. Since they were digging a large foundation right next to my building, there were risks involved so I needed to make sure there was someone looking out for my best interests. The contracts spelled out all the monitoring equipment that would be placed at my property. It specified how often they would be checked, movement thresholds, the works. All these costs were being paid for by the developer.

When we were almost done with the paperwork, they had an architecture firm come and draft up the exact square feet for the transaction. He came back with the 1,867 square feet. I contested this and spelled out my case for why I felt I owned additional development space. I got my zoning attorney on the phone and we went back and forth with the developer. They agreed to have their architect review everything. I held my breath for two weeks waiting to find out the verdict. Was I going to get the additional 40%, which would be a huge pay day? Or would they push back? I am not an architect and even my zoning attorney wasn't quite sure what the answer would be.

I felt I had a strong case here, but an expert needed to weigh in on the final decision and it wasn't my expert, it was theirs. Finally, we got the verdict from the architect. After careful review of the zoning regulations and survey, they concurred that I was correct and had an additional 730 square feet of development space, which they purchased at the same price per square foot. This was a massive win! Now the champagne corks could really fly.

KEYSTONE CONCEPT #17
Fight for Your Rights

Don't be afraid to stand up for what you believe to be correct, or what you honestly believe your property is worth. Do your math, stand behind your calculations, and be willing to fight for your rights. Sometimes they are worth a small fortune.

This air rights transaction was a windfall. For example purposes, let's call it $500,000. Erica and I were over the moon. We would be getting all the money we had put down on the building, including improvements, back in our pockets—plus a profit on top of that. That would make the cash-on-cash return of this property literally an infinite return because at this point, we would have no money in the property at all.

This was an awesome development, but what wasn't so great was the tax bill that would come along with the transaction. Here is how it would break out for us based on the tax rules in Massachusetts, where we were living at the time of the transaction:

20% capital gains tax

3.8% net investment tax

5.1% Massachusetts state tax

28.9% total in taxes

Invest now and pay the taxes later, if you possibly can

Ouch! Taxes are a part of life and I am certainly fine with paying my fair share of them but it definitely dilutes the amount of capital I would have available to invest in another project. Here is how it worked out for $500,000.

$500,000

$144,500 in taxes

$355,500 left to invest

But what if I didn't have to pay the taxes on this right now? What if I could defer the taxes until a later date? If I could do that, I would have nearly another $145,000 that I could invest (and would hopefully grow) and then I could pay the taxes on it later?

At the time of this transaction and the writing this book, there is something called a 1031 exchange which allows you to do just that. There has been talk in some political circles about removing this, so it may be eliminated in the future, who knows? Without getting into the weeds, there are two major points to understand about such a transaction.

1. It is a like-kind exchange. This means you need to sell something and buy something similar. So, if it is an investment property, you can exchange for a different investment property and defer paying the capital gains taxes that would normally be due. The replacement property needs to be the same or a higher price than the property you are exchanging, or you will need to pay taxes on the difference.

2. It is tax deferred. Not tax free. You will need to pay the taxes owed when you sell the new property. However, you can do another 1031 exchange on that property and buy another new property if you would like to. There is no limit on how many of these you can do. You can keep exchanging these for the rest of your life if you want. The purpose behind this is that the tax code is trying to encourage investors to keep providing properties. It incentivizes investors to keep their money in the real estate market rather than pulling it out. Make sense?

There is one case where the tax-deferral actually becomes tax-free and that is when you die. Morbid, I know. But when you die, the property passes to your heirs and something happens called a **step-up in basis**. I'm not going to teach accounting here, but essentially the basis is your cost in the property and it determines the profit you've made and will pay taxes on. When you do a 1031, the basis of the old property (subject to certain adjustments), becomes the basis of the new property, to account for the taxes you deferred on the first property. But when you die, the basis is "stepped up" to its fair market value, thus eliminating the tax on any appreciation of the property. For example, if you buy a property for $500,000 and sell it for $700,000, you would normally owe taxes on the $200,000 appreciation. But if your heir inherits the property instead, their cost basis would be stepped up to the current value of $700,000, which means they could sell the property at that price and not have any capital gain to pay taxes on.

Backstage Glossary

Step-Up in Basis: An adjustment to the value of an asset for tax purposes when it passes from an owner to their heir.

Timing is everything

There are strict timing requirements in order to complete a successful 1031 exchange. Remember, the government is incentivizing you to keep your money in the real estate market, so there are rules about how quickly you must re-invest to be able to defer your taxes. You must identify your replacement property (or properties) within 45 days of the closing of the sale of your property *and* you must close on the purchase of the replacement property within 180 days of the sale. If you miss either of these deadlines, the exchange is invalid and you cannot defer the taxes.

As a practical matter, 45 days is a very short period of time to identify replacement property. If you wait for the 45-day period, you are under a lot of pressure to find a suitable property and may end up overpaying for a property just to complete the exchange. If you are contemplating an exchange, you may want to start looking at your options before you put up your property for sale, which is exactly what I did. You can identify more than one property during the 45-day period, but you don't have to buy all of them. That gives you some flexibility to do additional due diligence on your options during the 45-day period.

Not only do you have these deadlines but you have to engage the services of a qualified intermediary (**QI**). The QI holds the proceeds from the sale and will disburse the proceeds on your behalf when you purchase your replacement property. In choosing a QI, it's worth the peace of mind to pay extra for an institutional QI so your sale proceeds are safe. A good QI will guide you through the entire process. Just as you have to meet the two deadlines, your exchange can also be at risk if the QI makes an error.

Backstage Glossary

QI: A Qualified Intermediary is someone who acts as an intermediary following certain sections of the U.S. Internal Revenue Code. They enter into a withholding agreement with the IRS and are allowed to facilitate certain types of transactions such as a 1031 exchange.

With all the rules and timing requirements, I wondered if it actually made sense for me to do this. I ran an analysis, assuming I would make an exchange, keep my investment in the new asset for at least ten years, and make a 10% annual return on the investment. Here's what I got:

10% compounded yearly for 10 years

$500,000 = $1,296,871 ($796,871 increase)

$355,500 = $922,075 ($566,575 increase)

The numbers showed I would make an additional $230,000 by using a 1031 exchange.

No brainer! What a win. It more than compensated for not getting the fireworks and marching band for my very first deal. This win was even better. I was starting to get the hang of what it took to make a purchase materialize like magic out of thin air. Now I needed to put all my new skills to work to pull this trick off, and pull that rabbit out of my hat.

CHAPTER 10 LESSONS LEARNED

- If you have the chance to defer taxes, take it, but make sure you know the fine print and follow the rules and regulations, or you could get stuck with a bigger tax bill *with interest*.

- If you own a property in a city, investigate your air rights situation, you could be sitting under a huge opportunity.

- Outdoor space is great, but Mother Nature requires regular care and maintenance or it might literally eat you alive.

- Stay alert to the fate of neighboring properties. Their destiny may impact your own.

REAL ESTATE TRICKS FOR MAGICIANS IN TRAINING

My transformational real estate magic act was only half complete. I was creating money out of thin air…literally. But this was only half the battle. It's like the magician sawed the assistant in half, but now the two pieces have to be put back together again, which is when the magic really happens. Leave them in two pieces, and that's not a magic act at all, it's carnage.

I was getting ready to sell the air rights on the Brooklyn property but would only be able to defer taxes through a 1031 exchange if I had a replacement property ready to go and meet the tight timing requirements. So, I stalled the final agreement on the sale while I started looking very quickly for the replacement property, before the clock started ticking.

I was living in Massachusetts and wanted to find something local. I didn't own any property in the state and while the laws there aren't too landlord friendly, I thought it would be good to own something in my backyard, if possible. From my limited local knowledge, I assumed I probably wasn't going to find anything that made sense, but wanted to give it a shot. I spent a couple frantic months looking for something, anything that was right and could be done quickly. Each time I came up empty-handed, so I started to turn my sights elsewhere.

Cultivate new connections

You would be surprised at the magic you can unlock when you go back over your mental rolodex and make a few calls that you have been putting off for a while. I had been stalling the sale of the property but that couldn't go on forever, they wanted to finalize the agreement and sign the documents.

After striking out looking for replacement property in my own area, and with the clock about to start ticking, I racked my brain for contacts in new markets that might be able to connect me quickly with an investment that made sense. That's when I remembered Brice. Back when I first began looking for properties in the Kansas City market, I came across a great broker named Brice. I had met him for breakfast one morning and he was an extremely nice person that I enjoyed speaking with. I had been on his email list since that time.

I was in KC to check in on Sunrise Properties and met with Brice. I explained that I was going to do a 1031 exchange, outlined my general timing, and told him what I was looking for. It turned out he knew someone who had a six-unit property that was going to be on the market in a couple of months. I asked Brice to speak with the owner about selling to me. I reviewed the financials, toured the property, and made an offer. It was accepted. Bing, bang, boom.

I am very conservative with my underwriting and would not have paid what I did for the property without the exchange. But when factoring everything in, it made sense for me to pay a slight premium to make sure I had this deal under contract around the time I signed the air rights agreement.

So, my timing worked out for the 1031 exchange. I closed on the sale of the air rights on December 26, identified the exchange property about a week later, and closed on the new property on February 12. All within the 1031 rules—a successful exchange and a release of pressure.

Still, I wanted to push the envelope just a little more to really flex my muscles and utilize all my real estate skills. I was going to implement a value-add on the new property, that was obvious, I always do that. But what about deprecation? I could utilize **bonus depreciation** to make this deal even more profitable.

Backstage Glossary

Bonus Depreciation: Allows you to deduct a large percentage of the purchase price of a property in the first year of ownership.

Learn how to make the depreciation of your assets work in your favor

Let's talk about depreciation because, as gloomy as it sounds, it's actually an important concept that can work in your favor. Depreciation is the reduction in the value of an asset over time. This is generally due to wear and tear on a property. When you have an investment property, you can get a certain amount of depreciation on it each year, based on the IRS rules.

Depreciation is captured as a loss. It can go against the property's income, and offset the taxes due. If the depreciation is equal to or more than the income generated from renting the property, you will not pay taxes on the income the property generates. Feeling a little bit cheerier on the topic of depreciation yet? Well, just wait. There's more.

Residential property depreciates over 27.5 years. You can depreciate the value of the physical building and other improvements, but you can't depreciate the value of the land. For example, let's say you purchase a property for $375,000 and the land itself is worth $100,000. Then you would have $275,000 to depreciate at a rate of $10,000 each year.

Pretty simple so far, right? Good.

Now, let's say for conversation's sake, that you had five units that rented for $500 a month. You would be generating $2,500 a month or $30,000 per year. If your expenses were $20,000 for the year, you would have a $10,000 profit from a cash perspective. However, due to the $10,000 depreciation, you would not owe any income taxes on the property that year.

How to turn up time

As you can see from the example, depreciating your property over 27.5 years can make a significant impact on your taxes. But what if you could do it faster? After all, does everything have a useful life of 27.5 years? Light bulbs, appliances, paint. Maybe you could keep the carpet for 27.5 years, but it would look pretty terrible.

The 27.5 years is for the building itself, but the personal property inside of it, along with the land improvements, all depreciate on their own schedules. You can hire a professional engineer to inspect your property and carefully document all the different types of property that depreciate at different rates.

The IRS has rules on how many years each of these items depreciate. The engineer catalogues all the items and matches them to the appropriate depreciation schedule. The end result is called a **Cost Segregation Study.** A tax preparer will then use this study when preparing the tax return for the owner(s) of the property. Some items will depreciate over five years, some seven, some fifteen, and so on. By using a cost segregation study, property owners can turn up time, accelerate depreciation, and gain more savings sooner rather than later.

> **Backstage Glossary**
>
> **Cost Segregation Study:** A report identifying the various components that make up a property as a whole, and their respective depreciation class lives. This is conducted by a qualified engineer and in compliance with U.S. tax and accounting rules.

Pump up the savings using bonus depreciation

The Tax Cuts and Jobs Act of 2017 that was passed by Congress made a lot of changes to the tax code in the United States. One of those changes was to allow all real estate investors having eligible assets to utilize something called bonus depreciation. This used to be something reserved for new construction and it had its own rules and limits. But with the new tax code, any property placed in service on or after September 27, 2017, can use bonus depreciation.

One of the options for bonus depreciation is that you can take everything that depreciates in 20 years or less, and depreciate all of this in the first year. Yes, you read that correctly. You can take 20 years' worth of depreciation and pull it all forward into the first year of ownership. This often ends up being 70% to 100% of the initial down payment on the property.

Now, before you get too excited about this, I want to make a couple of things very clear. First, it really depends on the property itself and you won't know how much bonus depreciation you can get until the study is conducted. Often, companies that perform these studies can give you an estimate. Secondly, this all depends on your tax situation. There are passive loss rules and you need to consult with a tax expert to see how this will apply to your specific situation. Unless you are a **real estate professional** or have some other large passive gain (i.e., from the sale of another property), the odds are that you will only be able to use a portion of those losses.

Backstage Glossary

Real Estate Professional: To reach this classification by the IRS, you must work 750 hours per year in real estate and you must work in this field more than any other work for the year. There are many additional nuances to this classification, so be sure to check with a qualified tax professional to see if it applies to you.

The good news is that whatever passive losses you don't use can be carried over into future years. Lastly, you need to know that there is such a thing as depreciation recapture that you may need to pay at the sale of a property. Bottom line here is that you need to *consult with your tax expert* about all of this and how it applies to your particular situation.

All that and a bucket of barbecue

I bought the new property all cash. So, the $500,000 I had made from the sale of the air rights was now sitting in my new six-unit property in Kansas City. And I left out the very best part. I have to confess that I *love* BBQ. I mean, I am really passionate about it. You might even say I'm a connoisseur. Ha!

One of the great things about all my trips to Texas and Kansas City has been the chance to try all the wonderful BBQ places. One of my favorite spots in Kansas City is called Q39. It's fantastic and I highly recommend it if you're in town. And when you do, be sure to look across the street and you'll see my 6-plex. That's right, the 6-unit property I bought just so happens to be across the street from one of my favorite places to eat. I'm not going to say that's why I bought it, the numbers made sense, but it surely didn't hurt and it sure beats being next to an abandoned KFC that breeds mosquitos by the trillions.

Do a cost segregation study sooner rather than later

As soon as we closed on the purchase of the property, I called the engineering firm to get the cost segregation study done. It's important to do the cost segregation early on in the project because if you segregate an item, say some carpet for example, and a few months later, the residents move out and you decide to replace it with tile, you have a record of that improvement. If you never captured the original carpet in the study, you are not able to depreciate it. This is a small example, but if this happens with many items, it can add up.

I reached out to a well-known engineering firm that does these studies. I had used another firm for the Sunrise deal and I wanted to try a different one so that I would have a couple of vendors on my list. We set up a kick-off call shortly after I closed on the property. I wanted to get this done right away to fully take advantage of any **partial asset disposition** that might occur. Partial asset disposition would allow me to write off the remaining useful life of any items that might be removed during renovation, and I knew that at some point I would be doing some renovations to add value to this property.

Backstage Glossary

Partial Asset Disposition: The removal of the remaining cost of a portion of an asset that is taken out of service. The remaining cost of the disposed assets produces a tax loss because that portion of the cost had not been deducted yet through depreciation.

The kick-off call included me, my CPA, and a team of three from the engineering firm—the account person, their assistant, and the engineer who would be performing the on-site inspection. We discussed the plan and the dates and were all set to go. The next day, the assistant called to ask for the closing statement on the purchase of the property, as they would need this to determine the basis for the property. I sent it over and she sent back an email saying that there was an issue since this was a 1031 exchange property and to send over the 1031 paperwork, which I did. I also called my accountant right away.

After a conversation with him, I realized there was something we'd missed. All of us on the kickoff call didn't think clearly through the entire thing. The issue was that with the specific nuances to my particular 1031 involving air rights *only*—not my entire property—my **depreciable basis** in the property was basically zero, yes you read that right, the big goose egg.

Backstage Glossary

Depreciable Basis: The amount of a fixed asset's cost that can be depreciated over time. This amount is the acquisition cost of the asset, which is the purchase price of an asset, plus the cost incurred to put the asset into service.

So, while I would be able to have bonus depreciation on this property, I was only able to depreciate against the basis of the property, which was essentially zero. My dreams of adding bonus depreciation as the cherry on top of my creative real estate sundae was thwarted. But I was still thrilled with my air rights to 1031 exchange. Now, there was one last trick up my sleeve.

And for a grand finale, refinance!

I owned my new property free and clear, but I had $500,000 sunk into it. It was cash-flowing like crazy because I had no debt payment, but all that money was tied up in the property. What I was able to do was a cash-out refinancing of the property. This is when you can get a loan from the bank on a property and wind up with cash in your pocket. Since this is a loan from the bank that you need to repay, it's not taxable income. I made sure to speak with my CPA about the timing of taking cash out through refinancing after completing a 1031 exchange and highly recommend anyone who wants to do this check with theirs too. I ended up getting a loan from a local bank for $400,000 which was 80% of the value of the property. This $400,000 was not taxable.

KEYSTONE CONCEPT #18

Refinance Responsibly Whenever You Can

Not all debt is bad. In fact, some debt can be downright profitable. Refinancing is a great way to reclaim stored equity in a property and deploy that capital into new investments that can produce more passive income. It can help you achieve your goals faster and, best of all, since you are borrowing the money, it is not considered income and you won't pay taxes on it.

If you look at the entirety of what I did over the course of time, instead of making $500,000 on the sale and paying $145,000 in taxes, leaving me with $355,000 to invest, I now had $100,000 in equity in a cash flowing property in Kansas City, and $400,000 in cash to invest in other projects. Through utilizing a 1031 exchange I ended up with an additional $45,000 of cash to invest that I wouldn't have had if I had paid taxes *plus* I had another property. (And a few extra pounds from too much BBQ!)

And one more time for emphasis: *read your documents*

There is a lesson to be learned about the refinance. It seems simple but please make sure you read all your documents carefully. You might be amazed how many people don't. Remember, we went over this in Chapter

9 with the loan documents for that transaction, where they just provided the signature pages. In the case of this deal, I was using a local lender. They sent me their boilerplate document and I was surprised when I read it.

Principal	Loan Date	Maturity	Loan No	Call / Coll	Account	Officer	Initials

References in the boxes above are for Lender's use only and do not limit the applicability of this document to any particular loan or item. Any item above containing "***" has been omitted due to text length limitations.

Borrower: Lender:

Principal Amount: Date of Note:

PROMISE TO PAY.   ("Borrower") jointly and severally promise to pay to ("Lender"), or order, in lawful money of the United States of America, the principal amount of Dollars (   ), together with interest on the unpaid principal balance from   , until paid in full.

PAYMENT. Borrower will pay this loan in full immediately upon Lender's demand. If no demand is made, subject to any payment changes resulting from changes in the index, Borrower will pay this loan in accordance with the following payment schedule, which calculates interest on the unpaid principal balances as described in the "INTEREST CALCULATION METHOD" paragraph using the interest rates described in this

See where it says, "Borrower will pay this loan in full immediately upon Lender's demand?" This didn't sit right with me. Obviously, if I was in default for not making a payment or something like that, they could accelerate the payments and make it due upon demand. That is fairly standard and was written elsewhere in the document. But the way this was written, they could, at any time, for any reason, or no reason, demand that I pay it back in full. I was not comfortable with this.

I reached out to the president of the bank to discuss. It sounds fancy that I'm talking with the bank president, right? He was an important bank official but it wasn't like I was chatting with Jamie Dimon at JPMorgan Chase. It was a small boutique bank, and I loved the sound of staying local with the financing. I wanted a bank that was as invested as I was in the vitality of the town.

I told him about the wording and my concerns. He told me that it was the boilerplate the bank has been using for years. He hadn't actually re-read it in years because no client had ever said anything about it, but that he would review it. When he did, he agreed that what I was saying was correct. I asked him if that could be changed and he went to the legal department and ultimately, they were willing to remove the language I didn't like.

I am telling you this to make sure you remember these two things:

1. *Read all documents* and understand what they mean before you sign them.

2. If you don't like the way something is written, ask to change it.

There are certain instances when documents can't be changed. But it never hurts to try. And if you don't feel comfortable with the terms, you can walk away. I would not have signed the documents if they refused to change them. I would have gone elsewhere.

One more thing I want to share with you. It's commonly referred to as the "Due on Sale Clause." This is standard and is in most mortgages. If you own your home, take a look through your mortgage and you will likely find something like this in it. It says that any change of the property's ownership makes the mortgage due immediately. This can be an issue if you owned a property in your name and then wanted to transfer the title to something else, like maybe a company that you own. Technically, you are not allowed to do that, and the lender can say that you now need to pay them in full for the mortgage. Here is what it looked like in our mortgage:

DUE ON SALE - CONSENT BY LENDER. Lender may, at Lender's option, declare immediately due and payable all sums secured by this Deed of Trust upon the sale or transfer, without Lender's prior written consent, of all or any part of the Real Property, or any interest in the Real Property. A "sale or transfer" means the conveyance of Real Property or any right, title or interest in the Real Property; whether legal, beneficial or equitable; whether voluntary or involuntary; whether by outright sale, deed, installment sale contract, land contract, contract for deed, leasehold interest with a term greater than three (3) years, lease-option contract, or by sale, assignment, or transfer of any beneficial interest in or to any land trust holding title to the Real Property, or by any other method of conveyance of an interest in the Real Property. However, this option shall not be exercised by Lender if such exercise is prohibited by federal law or by Missouri law.

We knew we wanted to transfer the title over to an entity, so we got the following clause added to our contract which explicitly states that we can transfer it over to an entity and that it will not trigger the due on sale clause.

COLLATERAL. Borrower acknowledges this Note is secured by
(1) A Deed of Trust from ▓▓▓ to Lender dated ▓▓▓ in the amount of ▓▓▓, to be recorded in Jackson County, Missouri, granting a security interest in the property legally described therein and commonly known as ▓▓▓, Kansas City, MO 64111: Lender consents to a deed transfer from ▓▓▓ to ▓▓▓ and said transfer will not trigger an acceleration of the debt per the Due on Sale clause in the Deed of Trust of ▓▓▓; and
(2) An Assignment of Rents from ▓▓▓ to Lender dated ▓▓▓, to be recorded in Jackson County, Missouri, granting a security interest as described therein, as they relate to the property legally described therein and commonly known as ▓▓▓ Kansas City, MO 64111.

Adding value

Now that I had the property, it was time to get down to business and implement the value add. During due diligence on the property, the residents were given a few days' notice that inspections of the units were going to take place so I could see what they looked like inside. Five of them were in good shape; maybe they could use a bit of an upgrade here or there but, overall, they were in good condition. Then there was that other one, one of the two-bedroom units.

Entering this unit with the inspection team was sort of a blur to me. There were a lot of people there. I remember there was someone passed out on the couch—this was at mid-day during the week. The unit itself was a shambles: filthy and disgusting. The unit had a washer and dryer and the dryer had been ruined. It looked like a tent or something had been put in there and melted inside the machine.

These residents had been in the unit for a few years. Their rent was below market and below the rent of the other two-bedroom unit in the building, even though this unit was a little larger and could be nicer than the others.

I knew that whenever these residents moved out, we could do a nice renovation on the unit and achieve much higher rent. I would never kick them out, but I thought that within a few years they might move out on their own.

As fate would have it, the day after I closed on the property, they stopped paying rent. My property management team spoke with them about this several times over the course of a few months. We asked if they were having a hardship, if we could work out a payment plan, if there was anything we could do to help them. We never got a response and, unfortunately, had to bring them to court. They were evicted from the property. This was unfortunate. It was not something we wanted to do and was certainly our last course of action.

After they moved out, we had a crew come in and clean the unit. I went to the property and talked with a contractor and pointed out some places where we could make some modifications to walls and door openings to make the place more open. I had them renovate the entire unit. New kitchen, new floors, paint. On the next page are some before and after pictures to give you an idea of the changes we made.

Entryway: Before

Entryway: After

Hallway & Living Room: After

Hallway & Living Room: Before

Kitchen: Before

Kitchen: After

The renovations were not cheap. The unit was a disaster and we had to replace the hardwood floors. We even removed portions of walls. Factoring everything in, the cost for this unit was $19,121.

The previous rent for the unit had been $900 but we knew we would be able to rent the renovated unit for $1,195—an increase of $295 per month.

The increase in rent would pay for the renovation in a little over 5 years.
$19,121 / $295 = 65 months (5.4 years)

But here is where the magic comes in.

Remember our formula for value:
NOI / Cap Rate = Value

We increased our NOI by $295 per month for a total of $3,540
$295 X 12 = $3,540 per year

And an extremley conservative cap rate for the area is 6%.

So, if we plug that into our valuation formula, we can see that we increased the value of the property by $59,000.
$3,540 / .06 = $59,000

After removing the renovation costs, we have about $40,000 in profit.
$59,000 - $19,000 = $40,000

This is a return on investment of 210%!

We didn't renovate any other units in the building during that time period (and none of them were in need of such an extensive renovation). One thing we did do was work with a local entrepreneur who is using one of the studio apartments as a short-term rental. He signed a lease with us that is about $200 more per month than the standard market rent (which we are getting for the other studio) and he is renting the unit for short-term stays through websites such as Airbnb or Vrbo.

I am happy to collect $200 more per month than I would otherwise. He is happy to do all the work dealing with tenants, cleaning the unit, and taking on the risk of vacancy. He makes a nice profit from his work. Another great win-win scenario!

CHAPTER 11 LESSONS LEARNED

- Cultivate new connections by reviewing your old rolodex. You will be surprised who you know and forgot you knew.

- Learn how to make depreciation your friend by turning up time and using bonus depreciation.

- Don't overlook the lifestyle perks. They have value also.

- Do a cost segregation study as soon as you can so that you can monetize your improvements.

- Improvements enhance the quality of life for your tenants and the bottom line.

- Sidehacks like Airbnb and entrepreneurial tenants can increase profit for both of you. Don't automatically rule out these opportunities if you have a reliable and enterprising tenant.

A WORK IN PROGRESS

My adventures in real estate started when I bought that first co-op in New York City out of necessity and came up with the idea that I could reinvent property ownership as a positive for communities. I also wanted some control over how I spent my time, the decisions I had to make, and since I had lost my apartment unexpectedly, I wanted some certainty about where I was going to live.

Fast forward 20 years, and I now own several thousand apartment units, but the important thing to understand is that 65% of my investment portfolio are deals in which I am strictly a passive investor. The other 35% of my portfolio contains deals that I actively manage. As a result of my diverse investment history, I've seen deals from all sides of the equation. I sponsor deals now for my own discreet group of investors and I have many plans on my dashboard for the future. My portfolio and I are a work in progress. And I love that.

As a passive investor, I've cultivated a diversified portfolio of investments that provide me with cash flow on a regular basis and leave me at liberty to do the things I care about every day. It also gives me the opportunity to put my dollars to work in the world in ways that are important to me.

My wife works in the entertainment field. She enjoys being part of both the business and the creative aspects of bringing the arts to the public. I share her passion for the arts and the transformative power of theater to bolster social change. While Erica gets to do this in her day-to-day work, I am fortunate enough to have joined her in some theatrical pursuits that have gone beyond her daily work.

We were able to invest in iconic shows like *Hamilton*, which, with its diverse cast and fresh perspective on history, has become a landmark in pop culture. We are proud to have received our first Tony awards as co-producers of David Byrne's *American Utopia* where the Talking Heads frontman was joined by an ensemble of 11 musicians, singers, and dancers from around the globe. This amazing and important production invited its audience into a joyous dreamworld where human connection, self-evolution, and social justice hold sway. We won our second Tony Awards as co-producers of *Moulin Rouge! The Musical* a show that champions the ideals of truth, beauty, freedom, and love!

While investments in Broadway shows are disproportionally risky, they can also have an asymmetric return. Due to this risk, we are very cautious about the shows we choose to be involved with. But when it is something that we feel passionate about, we do get involved and sometimes extend the opportunity to a select group of my real estate investing friends. We have all found it interesting that most Broadway shows are structured in syndications, just like real estate deals.

The opportunity to merge my first love of the arts with my current passion for real estate is so special to me, and I have discovered it's integral to my sense of well-being and personal fulfillment. In both cases, while there is commercial interest, I do my best to be involved in projects that matter, that aim to help society move forward, that start a conversation beautifully—a conversation that we as a society and a global community need to have. With all of my investments, I try to leave things a little better than I found them.

I hope I've done the same with this book. I worked hard to share as many of the things that I've learned in the world of real estate investing that I believe are necessary to helping you grasp the industry and to take note of the small but crucial details that can make or break you. I hope to leave you a little better off than when I found you, and better equipped to take the same journey toward financial freedom that I have, though hopefully without having to learn so many lessons the hard way like I did.

I think these two pictures sum up my adventure. Remember this picture from Chapter 2? It's me in front of our apartment on the morning before my first day of preschool.

Oakwood Village – 1976

I lived here with my family until I was around five. Some of my first memories of life are from moments at this apartment. My sister was born when we lived there.

Now, this is a photo of me 44 years later in front of that same door except for one big difference.

LIV @ Winter Park – 2020

Instead of renting the apartment, I'm an owner of the complex. I'm not sure that the younger me would completely understand this, but I bet he would think it's pretty cool.

And as a final full-circle moment, do you remember from the first chapter that we bridged the gap from Brooklyn to Miami, keeping the townhome and our options open? Well, Erica got another one of those famous calls and we crossed back over that Brooklyn Bridge during the summer of 2021 and moved back home to New York City.

Good luck on your own adventures in real estate investment. I wish you much success, but when you stumble, as we all do, don't forget to reach out to your trusted experts and be guided by their counsel. It is my hope that this book, and the advice in it, will become an integral part of that instrumental community.

And of course, I am always just an email away and look forward to hearing the story that you write.

Matt Picheny
matt@picheny.com

THE BACKSTAGE
TOOL BOX

QUICKLY SIZING UP
A SYNDICATION

I've learned that there are three things you need to consider when you're vetting a syndication deal. So, for ease of use, I have divided this quick guide into these three critical areas of concern:

The Sponsor

The Market

The Deal

Here are some questions to ask yourself about these three areas, along with a key for how to evaluate your answers. In each case, I'll list the good signs to look for (thumbs up icon), the signs that you might want to take a second look and ask questions before proceeding (fingers crossed), and the warning signs that tell you that you should turn around and run in the other direction (thumbs down).

The Sponsor

When considering any deal, you need to look first at who is running it. You can have a great deal in a fantastic market but if the sponsorship team doesn't know what they're doing, you're toast.

Vet who you are working with very carefully. Do your research before you invest, because if you invest, you're going to be handing them tens or even hundreds of thousands of your hard-earned dollars. Make sure that the sponsor is a good match for you.

I personally want a sponsor who shares my communication style, my management philosophy, and my values. Things to consider about the sponsor should include the following.

1. **How did you meet the sponsor?**

   Yes: Personal referral, preferably from someone who has invested with them before.

   Maybe: Someone you've found online who has been in the business for some time.

   Get Lost: An unsolicited email or social media message.

2. **What is their track record?**

   Yes: Has completed multiple "full cycle" deals with positive results.

   Maybe: Has multiple deals performing at, or close to, projections.

   Get Lost: This is their first deal, they have no experienced partners, but they just finished a great online program.

3. **Is compensation commensurate with experience?**

   Yes: Someone with a strong track record with fees in the 1% to 3% range and who retains 30% (or less) of equity in the deal.

   Maybe: Someone with a weaker track record but who is taking less equity and lower (or is eliminating) fees.

   Get Lost: Someone who has never done a deal before but is charging a large acquisition and other fees.

4. **Do you share the same investment philosophy?**

   Yes: You have had conversations with the sponsor and you are aligned.

👎 **Maybe:** You may have some variances of opinion but generally you agree.

👎 **Get Lost:** The sponsor can't articulate their philosophy or it's one you disagree with.

5. **What is their level of involvement?**

👍 **Yes:** Key decision maker, loan guarantor who has invested a significant amount of time and their own money in the deal.

👎 **Maybe:** Has a seat at the decision table and has personally invested the minimum amount in the deal or done significant work to acquire the deal.

👎 **Get Lost:** Solely raising capital for the deal, no seat at the table, and not listed in the legal documentation.

The Market

Location is often touted as the most important factor in real estate—and for good reason! All the smart decisions in the world can't change the location. Properties in great locations can perform well. Properties on the path of progress can do even better. But how do you evaluate the market? Here are some clues.

1. **Is the market poised for growth?**

👍 **Yes:** Above average population and employment growth.

👎 **Maybe:** Slow and steady population and employment growth.

👎 **Get Lost:** Declining population and employment.

2. **What are the employment opportunities?**

👍 **Yes:** Diverse employment across several different industry types.

👎 **Maybe:** At least three different major employers across three different industry types.

👎 **Get Lost:** A vast majority of employment is from one company.

3. **Does the area have strong demographics?**

👍 **Yes:** Residents have good income and education coupled with low crime and unemployment rates.

✋ **Maybe:** Average income and education, moderate crime and unemployment.

👎 **Get Lost:** High levels of crime and unemployment.

4. **Desirable area amenities?**

👍 **Yes:** An area filled with desirable grocery, shopping, medical, and other conveniences.

✋ **Maybe:** Moderate number of sought-after destinations in the immediate area with others within a short drive.

👎 **Get Lost:** Limited to no desirable amenities in the immediate area.

5. **Is this a place you would want to visit?**

👍 **Yes:** A nice, clean property in a city you would like to visit.

✋ **Maybe:** A good property in a place you wouldn't mind visiting.

👎 **Get Lost:** You would be afraid to visit the property on your own.

The Deal

Great leadership and a fantastic location don't stand a chance if the business plan is flawed. The devil is in the details. Looking at the strategy and mechanics of the deal can help you determine the chance of success.

1. **What is the business plan?**

👍 **Yes:** Force appreciation through a value-add program while cash flowing through ownership period.

✋ **Maybe:** Buy and hold for long-term cash flow.

> **Get Lost:** Sale or refinance in a short period of time, based solely on market appreciation.

2. **What type of debt will be used?**

> **Yes:** Long term, agency debt (Fannie Mae or Freddie Mac).

> **Maybe:** Carefully underwritten Bridge or CMBS Loan.

> **Get Lost:** Short term "hard money" loan.

3. **What types of metrics have been used to underwrite the deal?**

> **Yes:** Historical metrics provided by reputable publications.

> **Maybe:** Local market knowledge, verified by local third party.

> **Get Lost:** Based solely on selling broker's pro forma.

4. **Projected Returns?**

> **Yes:** Total return, IRR, and cash-on-cash are in line with your investment goals and based on a sound, conservative underwriting model that the sponsor can justify.

> **Maybe:** Expected returns are close to your targets and based on conservative expectations for rent growth and exit cap rate.

> **Get Lost:** Shows a high equity multiple but is based on a refinance, or aggressive underwriting with lofty assumptions.

5. **Fees and Compensation?**

> **Yes:** All fees and compensation are clearly disclosed, easy to understand and within industry norms.

> **Maybe:** Fees and compensation are complex but disclosed and within industry norms.

> **Get Lost:** Fees and compensation are confusing and above industry norms.

If you properly evaluate these three pillars, pay particular attention to who is leading the deal, do your research up front, and understand your values and goals, your passive investment can be a win-win. You can gain financial freedom and improve the quality of life for your investment communities, while minimizing your risk.

A BACKSTAGE TOUR OF SYNDICATIONS

At this point I think you've got a good understanding of the strategy and general mechanics of syndication. At least I hope you do after reading this book! Now, if you're ready to take the next step, here are some nuts and bolts of advanced deal analysis that you may find helpful.

I'll explore some of the levers that people who are putting together a syndication can pull. These are things that they can either dial up or dial down to make a deal look more attractive or seem less risky than it actually is. The goal here is to give you an insider's perspective about how these deals work. This is a chance to look behind the curtain and see what's going on in the inner workings, so you can invest or not invest with your eyes wide open. There are a lot of concepts here; I've laid them out in no particular order.

Securities

Any investment that is sold in the United States is considered a **security**, and in order to legally sell a security that person needs to be a registered broker-dealer. This means the person has to have a license and register with the securities and exchange commission. In addition, the investment must be registered as well. It takes considerable time and money to register securities, so much so that you probably won't be able to complete a registration in the amount of time you have available to close on a real estate deal. Most real estate syndication sponsors do not have a broker-dealer license. Without the time to register the investment, and without a broker-dealer license, most sponsors utilize an exemption in the SEC code called Regulation D.

> ### ── Backstage Glossary ──────────
>
> **Security:** A financial instrument that holds monetary value. It can be in the form of equity, debt, or a hybrid, and is regulated by the SEC.

Regulation D

The Securities and Exchange Commission (SEC) is a part of the federal government that was created following the 1929 stock market crash to protect investors. The SEC has a regulation called **Regulation D** that allows for some exemptions to what is considered a security. If you follow the rules, you can have a private offering that is not considered a security, and it's therefore perfectly legal for you to have these offerings. There are a few subsections under Regulation D and most syndications fall under 506(b) or 506(c).

> ### ── Backstage Glossary ──────────
>
> **Regulation D:** A Securities and Exchange Commission regulation that allows a project to be considered exempt from having to be registered as a security with the SEC.

506(b)

A **506(b)** offering can be offered only to people who have a preexisting and substantive relationship with the sponsor. If a sponsor has a deal under contract, they can't meet someone for the first time and in that same moment offer this investment—that would be violating the rules. They have to have met the person prior to getting the property under contract. Also, the relationship must be substantive—they can't have just met the person at a crowded networking event, received their card, and started emailing them deals. They need to follow up with that person, get to know them, understand their financial situation, and learn about their investment goals and risk tolerance.

Backstage Glossary

506(b): A subsection of SEC Regulation D that allows for accredited and up to 35 sophisticated investors to participate in exempt offerings, provided the investor has a preexisting substantive relationship with the sponsor.

The other stipulation around this type of offering is that it is open to both accredited and up to 35 **sophisticated investors**. An accredited investor as defined by the SEC is: A person with an individual or joint net worth (with a spouse) of more than $1 million, excluding their primary residence. Or, someone who in each of the last two years has had an individual income in excess of $200,000—or a joint income (with a spouse) in excess of $300,000—and reasonably expects to continue to reach that income level. As of August 2020, the SEC also defined measures of professional knowledge, experience, or certifications in addition to the tests for income or net worth. A sophisticated investor is not as clearly defined by the SEC. It is someone who understands how to look at real estate deals, evaluate them and understands the risk involved with such an investment.

Backstage Glossary

Sophisticated Investor: Someone with sufficient knowledge and experience in financial and business matters to make them capable of evaluating the merits and risks of the prospective investment. Unlike an accredited investor, the SEC does not have financial thresholds to meet this status.

506(c)

With this kind of offering, only accredited investors may participate. The investor's accredited status needs to be verified by a third party such as a CPA or attorney. The trade-off here is that a **506(c)** offering can be advertised because a preexisting substantive relationship is not required. A 506(c) offering can be presented to someone right when a sponsor meets them.

Backstage Glossary

506(c): Subsection of SEC Regulation D that allows for only accredited investors to participate in exempt offerings.

Legal Documentation

The sponsors have an attorney set up the syndication with the following items:

1. They create a single purpose entity that will acquire the property.

2. The legal team creates an operating agreement for the entity. That operating agreement contains the rules the entity will follow throughout all of the business's operations.

3. The legal team creates a PPM, which is a Private Placement Memorandum. This goes into more detail on the structure of how the entity will function and how it conforms to SEC rules. Inside the private placement memorandum there are lots of warnings; it calls out many of the things that could go wrong with the deal. It also has disclosures on fees, the operating agreement, and the structure on which this business is going to run.

4. There is a subscription agreement, which documents the amount of ownership the investor is purchasing in the entity.

5. There is usually an investor questionnaire, which asks the investor several questions to ascertain whether they are sophisticated or accredited. Or, if it is a 506(c) offering, there is an affidavit that must be signed by a CPA or attorney, verifying the investor's accredited status.

6. Finally, there is often a business plan in the form of a PowerPoint presentation which describes the sponsor's plan and how the company will be profitable.

Life Cycle of a Deal

1. A sponsor finds a property, gets it under contract, and then reaches out to their investors.

2. They let the investors know about the offering and send out the legal documents for review. Often, they conduct an online presentation to discuss the offering.

3. Investors complete the paperwork and then fund that investment.

4. The sponsors close on the deal and then operate the deal.

5. The property is sold, hopefully providing the projected results.

Business Plan

Make sure that you have a clear understanding of the sponsor's business plan, and make sure it is well-articulated: a misunderstanding on the plan is the last thing you want. A cohesive, well-articulated business plan detailing exactly what a sponsor is planning to do with the property is essential and should be included as an exhibit to the legal documents. Will it be a buy and hold? How long will you be in this investment? Are they looking to add value? Perhaps they are just going to operate the property more efficiently?

Whatever the strategy, you want to make sure it's written down and that it makes logical sense at a high level. Since you essentially have no control over the operations of the company, you are putting your faith in the sponsor(s). Making sure you're aligned with the business plan at the beginning is important in ensuring there's no confusion once the property is acquired.

Manager Removal

A limited partner basically has no control over the entity, but there is one clause I look for in all the deals I invest in. While I don't have any control over the day-to-day operations, most of the good operating agreements, in my opinion, are ones that do allow for the manager to be removed. If a majority of the limited partners feel that the person who is managing the property is not managing it well, they should have the power to go ahead and remove the person from office and bring in a new manager.

Capital Calls

Another thing I always want to understand is how a **capital call** would be handled. A capital call is when the entity needs funding and reaches out to the members for that money. While this, hopefully, is never going to happen, I have seen cases where, for one reason or another, a company needs some additional funding.

> ### — Backstage Glossary —
>
> **Capital Call:** When a syndication asks members to contribute capital into the company. Depending on the operating agreement, these can be mandatory or discretionary.

The operating agreement should explain how capital calls, however unlikely, will be handled. If you contribute to the capital call, then everything is fine, but what happens if you can't or don't want to contribute? Discretionary capital calls (in the majority of syndications, but not all) are capital calls requested by the manager or general partner asking for additional capital. There will be dilution for those that do not participate (usually very minimal, depending on the total capital raised and the additional amount of capital needed); however, there is no penalty associated with these. Mandatory capital calls are capital calls that are mandatory (just as the name implies) such that when the manager or general partner requires additional capital, members/limited partners that do not participate are typically diluted and penalized. I have seen agreements where, if you don't participate in a capital call, you can actually lose your entire investment. I don't invest in deals like that because I don't think they are fair. If I don't (or can't) contribute additional capital, I think it's fine that my interest would be diluted, but I shouldn't lose my entire investment.

Tax Partnerships

All of the deals I have invested in are taxed as a partnership. This means the company files a tax return at the end of the year and provides me with a K1 that shows my portion of any profits or losses in the company. The company does not pay corporate tax, the portion of tax equal to my ownership is reflected in the K1 document, and I use that when filing my tax return. Because of depreciation, as we discussed at length in Chapter 11, these K1s usually provide me with some tax savings during the time that we own the property.

Sponsor Fees

There are so many variables involved in getting a deal under agreement. It can take years to learn a market, develop the right relationships, find an opportunity, and negotiate the deal. The sponsors have to put forth a significant amount of capital to get an opportunity to the point where they are presenting it to investors. This includes earnest money deposits, inspections fees, legal fees, loan applications, etc. Then the asset needs to be managed properly to execute the business plan. Syndicators need to be compensated for all of this hard work, but you want to make sure that the compensation is commensurate with their experience and with the returns they've produced for investors in the past.

There are essentially three typical types of fees that sponsors could receive from a syndication.

1. **Acquisition Fee:** This is the fee that the sponsorship group is going to get upon closing the deal. As you now know, there is a lot of hard work and expense involved in putting something like this together: this is how to compensate them for that work. Acquisition fees are typically a percentage of the purchase price and they generally range between 1% and 3%. I am fine with paying a modest acquisition fee to someone with a proven track record. I have declined to invest in deals with a brand-new sponsor team that had no experience and were asking a 3% acquisition fee. While sponsors deserve to be compensated for their hard work, I don't think a new sponsor should make a large sum of money before they have produced a dime for investors.

2. **Disposition or Capital Events Fee:** This fee is charged either on the sale or on the refinance of a property. It's a fee that that the sponsorship takes that's generally between 1% and 3%. While acquisition fees are quite common, disposition/capital event fees are less so.

3. **Asset Management Fee:** This fee compensates the sponsorship team for overseeing the property. While there is often a property management company handling the day-to-day operations (rent collections, maintenance, leasing), someone should be overseeing this from the owner's perspective. On all the deals where I am the asset manager, I have weekly calls with my property management companies and we review the finances on a monthly basis. I also share all of that information with the investors monthly, so there are a multitude of activities happening. I generally see an asset management fee of anywhere from 1% to 3% of the revenue collected each month.

Carried Interest or Sweat Equity

This is the percentage of the deal that the sponsors will retain for themselves in exchange for all their efforts on the project. This can be a big payday for them and happens after a property is sold, which can be several years after the purchase. The numbers can vary greatly on this; I've seen it go from certain sponsors taking 10% off the top to some taking 50% or more. I prefer investing in deals that have a set amount, but I have seen deals structured in a "waterfall" where, once certain metrics are hit, the sponsors' percentage increases.

Distributions to investors are typically sent on a monthly or quarterly basis. These distributions of cash flow are subject to the investor/sponsor split. Generally, I don't invest in deals that give the investors less than 70% of the equity in a deal. Ultimately though, I honestly don't care if a sponsor is getting a higher percentage of the deal (if they have a strong track record). What I care about is what my return is going to look like at the end of the day. I look to double my money in five to seven years and to have strong cash flow (preferably double digits) during the time we own the property.

Preferred Return

This is when a certain percentage of the cash flow distributions are designated to go only to the investors. The preferred return is paid before the sponsors participates in any of the cash flow. For example, let's say you invest in a deal with an 80/20 split and an 8% preferred return. In year one, the property only distributed 7.5% in cash flow. All of that cash flow would go to the Investors, none to the sponsors. But if the deal had 12% to distribute, investors would get 9.6% and since the 8% threshold had been met, the sponsors would get the remaining 2.4%.

Return on Capital vs Return of Capital

The little change of "on" vs "of" can make a big difference on the investors share of the profits on a deal, and you need to be aware of this. In a "return of capital" scenario, the amount you invested in the deal, which is known as your "capital account" is reduced by the amount of every distribution. So, if you invested $100,000 in a deal and received $50,000 in distributions over the course of the deal, you would have $50,000 remaining in your capital account. If the deal was then sold, you would get the $50,000 remaining in your capital account returned to you before the investor/sponsor split started. In a "return on capital" structure, your $100,000 capital account would remain steady at that amount. The $50,000 you received in distributions would not reduce your capital account. So, at the sale, you would receive $100,000 before the investor/sponsor split started.

Backstage Glossary

Return of Capital: Returns received by the investor *are* deducted from their capital account.

Return on Capital: Returns received by the investor *are not* deducted from their capital account.

Clearly the return on capital structure is more advantageous to the investor. Don't let this one little thing throw you off too much. Almost every deal I have invested in has been a return of capital structure. Also, most of those deals have a 20% sponsor compensation model vs 30%. I modeled a scenario in which someone invests $100,000 on a deal that lasts five years, and receives a 10% distribution of the initial investment every year. In this model, using return on capital and a 70/30 split, the investor's total profit was $99,000. Using the same model, but a return of capital and an 80/20 split, the investor's total profit was $98,000. As you can see, these are nearly the same.

The Four Fudgeable Factors

There are four different factors that can really move the needle on a deal. I call them "The Fudgeable Four" because they can be easily changed a little and just this slight change can make a big difference to the deal.

These are the items I want to dig deep into when I'm reviewing the underwriting of a deal to make sure I understand how the sponsor came up with the numbers. Since a lot of them are assumptions, I want to make sure I agree with them.

All the items I'll mention are red flags to me, things I would question, though sponsors might have different and very justifiable responses to them. Your deal sponsor might have a great reason why they have underwritten the deal the way that they did. I am just bringing to your attention things that might be a little out of the ordinary—things you might want to bring up with the sponsor and discuss. They should be able to explain to you exactly why a particular item is different than you were expecting and what their thinking is. Then you can make the decision as to whether you agree with them and whether you like the investment or not.

Before we dive in, let's talk about the financial modeling that you should get from the deal sponsor. Sponsors can present information to their investors in many different ways. Sometimes sponsors give you a lot of information and in other situations you get very little. I've heard people say that the riskier a deal is, the more information will be provided. This implies that a really good sponsor with a good track record doesn't need to give the information to their investors. I disagree with this approach. While too much information can be overkill, I think there are fundamental pieces of information that should be given to investors no matter what a sponsor's track record is. I personally won't invest in a deal without looking at them.

Among the things that I always want to see are the **T12** and **T3** on the deal. The T stands for "trailing." The T12 is the trailing 12 months of profit and loss on the property, broken down by month. These financial statements can give you a good understanding of the financial performance of a property during that time.

Backstage Glossary

T12: A financial report showing the trailing 12 months of profit and loss, broken down by month. The trailing 3 months is referred to as the T3.

A T3 is often stronger, especially if the owner has been tightening up operations and increasing rents. You always want to look at the T12, not just a T3, because there are certain expenses that are seasonal, or only come up once or twice a year and those will be captured in the T12. These are items like property tax and insurance, which can be quite expensive and really skew the numbers.

Fudgeable Factor #1: Cap Rates

We looked at cap rates back in Chapter 8 when we discussed how to value a property. NOI / Cap Rate = Value. You may remember from the earlier valuation discussion that there is an inverse relationship between values and cap rates. As a cap rate goes up, it means the value goes down. The cap rate is a crucial part of the formula that's going to determine the value of a property at purchase, but most importantly when a property is sold.

You may also remember that cap rates are a good way to value a property because they show the returns that could be achieved without factoring in any debt. This allows you to have a true "apples to apples" comparison of how different properties perform, irrespective of any debt placed on the property, which can vary greatly.

In the sponsor's pro forma, they will have an assumed cap rate at the time of sale. This will be called something like an exit cap rate, terminal cap rate, or reversion cap rate—they all mean the same thing. The sponsor uses this assumed cap rate, along with the expected NOI, to determine the anticipated value of the property at the time of sale.

The thing you need to understand is that even a little change to that cap rate can have a dramatic effect on your sales price. A shift of a quarter of a point can have massive influence on the property's valuation. When I sponsor a deal, I like to present a cap rate sensitivity study, like the one below, which illustrates the projected return over time based on different exit cap rates. In the deal illustrated below, if we were to exit in year four with a 7.0 cap rate, the investor's return would be over 91%. However, with just a half point change to 7.5, the return is lowered to 65%.

Total Return

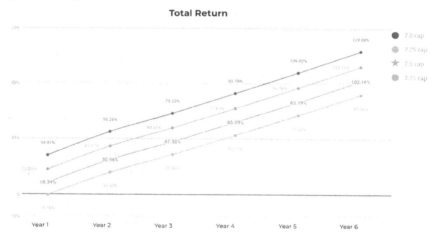

When looking at the cap rates, I like to have a good understanding of the purchase cap rate. I can do this by looking at the T12 or T3, but the T12 is going to be more accurate. In the example above, we bought the property at a 6.0 cap rate according the T12. You should take note that in the chart's legend the 7.5 cap rate is represented by a star. This was our projected exit cap rate.

We bought at a 6 cap, which was the prevailing rate in this submarket at the time that we acquired the property. This was in mid 2018, when the real estate market was super-hot and everybody wanted to get involved, especially with multifamily properties. People were paying extraordinary amounts of money for properties, so a 6 cap was the going rate, however, when I dug into the historical data on this submarket, I saw that the cap rates were usually between 7.25 and 7.5. We had projected holding the property for five years and my feeling was that cap rates would not stay so compressed forever.

There is a financial theory called **mean reversion** which states that, over time, asset prices always revert to the mean. Markets go up and markets go down but, ultimately, they revert to the long-term average. In a really hot real estate market, where cap rates are compressed, you get low rates. My belief is that they will go back up. Conversely, in a market where real estate prices are low, cap rates may be artificially high and you could write an exit cap rate that's lower. I take this into account with all my forecasting. I look at the historical data and base my cap rate on this information. In this case, I took a conservative approach and set our exit cap rate at 7.5.

Backstage Glossary

Mean Reversion: Also known as reversion to the mean, this is a financial theory that states that asset prices and volatility of returns eventually revert to their long-term average levels.

A word of caution: *no one* can reliably predict these things. I try to underwrite deals with an abundance of caution. The property in this example was sold at a 6.75 cap rate, which is .75 lower than we had projected. We were happy to hit our goals and achieve our objectives faster than we had anticipated, but we were fortunate that we had the strong tailwinds of the market behind us. We were prepared for rougher market conditions.

In a hot real estate market, cap rates can be compressed, yet I'll see people underwriting these deals where the exit cap rate is the same as their purchase cap rate, or only marginally higher or, in some cases, even lower! I think that brings a tremendous amount of risk to the deal. When you're trying to forecast for five to ten years from now, I'm not sure that cap rates are going to be the same, or lower, when they are already at historic lows.

I was at a conference and heard a major sponsor, who has a ton of property, speak. The sponsor was underwriting deals with the current cap rates for their exits in five to ten years, and said they were doing so because they believed that interest rates were going to continue to move down. Rates were at historic lows and, while I don't have a crystal ball, I didn't feel comfortable making a similar prediction. Maybe I'll end up being wrong, but I think betting someone else's money that rates are going to continue to go down, when they are already at historic lows, is pretty bold. And more than that, the sponsor is selling a false narrative: that cap rates are directly tied to interest rates. They are saying, "The interest rates are going down, therefore the cap rate will go down too."

While historically, over very long periods of time, cap rates tend to follow the same general trend as interest rates, they are not in lockstep. As the chart below illustrates, the spread between interest and cap rates can vary widely. For example, look how the 10-year treasury dropped between 2006 and 2012. Cap rates went up during that period of time and the spread between the two grew by 380 bps. The data simply doesn't support the statement that cap rates move directly with interest rates.

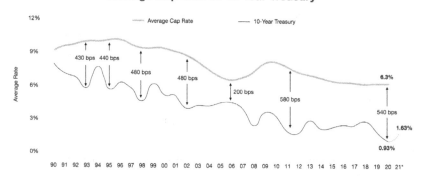

U.S. Commercial Real Estate Yield Spread Widens
Average Cap Rate vs 10-Year Treasury

In conclusion, know what cap rate the property is being purchased at and understand where the sponsor believes cap rates will be at the time of sale. That exit cap rate has a huge effect on the projected final return. Make sure your sponsor can justify that cap rate. Ask if they have any third-party data that shows historical cap rates—not just from the past few years where the market has been great. If they don't have third-party data backing up their cap rate hypothesis, I really would want a good explanation from them.

Fudgeable Factor #2: Income Growth

One of the biggest factors that's going to drive any pro forma is income growth. If an increase in income is projected, the returns can look fantastic. But is this growth achievable? There are a number of different factors that impact a properties income. The three components that will affect total income growth are rent growth, other income growth, and vacancy.

Rent Growth

Most of the deals I look at have a value-add strategy. We see a significant lift in rents for renovated units. On top of that, there is natural growth in the market rent and this is also put into the underwriting model. When evaluating deals, as I've mentioned elsewhere in this chapter, I want to see third-party historical data that supports the assumptions. The market rent that is projected in the pro forma needs to be backed by data.

There are some hot markets right now where there has been rent growth of 5% to 10% in the past few years. That is fantastic, but when looking historically at that market, maybe it usually sees 2% growth. We've had a very strong economy and rent increases have been huge over the past five years or so, but will that continue? Are the people who live in the area, the residents, getting wage increases of 5% to 10% every year?

If you are looking at a pro forma that has modeled a 5% increase in rents each year, but employers around there are not increasing wages by that amount, at some point you are going to hit the ceiling and not be able to push rents higher. This illustrates how important it is to know who the people are that will make up the resident base and whether they're getting wage increases that match the rent increases, or you will price yourself out of the market. Make sure there is empirical evidence that supports the rent growth numbers. I think anything between 0% to 2% is probably okay, depending on the area, but once it starts going over 2%, I'd be very cautious. I'd want to see something supporting this aggressive growth.

Other Income

The same goes for "other income." This can be interesting in a value-add play where there are opportunities to increase other income. It's a smart business strategy to increase other income but just make sure it's on par with what other properties in the area are doing. Carports sound like a great idea, but if the other properties in the area have carports and are not charging for them, it's not going to be of value to add them to a property. I'm just using carports as an example, but the same principle goes for everything from utility bill backs to package lockers.

Vacancy

Last of all, there's vacancy. It's very important that we look at *economic* vacancy, not just physical vacancy. Physical vacancy is the number of units in your apartment complex that are not occupied. Economic vacancy is your potential income vs your actual income. Economic vacancy accounts for three items beyond physical occupancy: loss to lease, concessions, and bad debt.

Loss to lease is when you allow a long-term resident to stay at the property for a rent that is below market. Often, they are a great resident, they pay on time and never cause any problems. You let them stay in the unit because it would cost you a lot of money to turn the unit over and you would have vacancy of the unit during that time. It can make sense to let that person stay in the unit, even at the lower rental rate, because you save on the turn-over costs, including vacancy.

Concessions are any sort of specials you might have running at the property. These are usually incentives you create to maintain your physical occupan-cy. A concession might be a discount on rent, a free month, or something of that nature. At some of our properties, we offer discounts to military and police officers.

And then there's bad debt, which happens when a resident stops paying rent. Sometimes they stop paying and disappear. Other times, their non-payment continues and we have to go to court. In either event, the rent that is not paid goes on the financials as money owed—or debt. At a certain point, if we haven't collected those funds, they get sent to collections and are taken off the financials. They are written off in our accounting records as "bad debt," a debt that was never paid.

To determine projected economic occupancy, what I like to do is find his-torical data (are you seeing a pattern here?) for physical vacancy in that submarket and add an additional 3% on top of that for loss to lease, con-cession, and bad debt. Sometimes I adjust that 3% up or down a little, depending on the property and submarket.

Total income increase

From my experience, I don't think it's practical to project an increase of total income on a property of more than 10% a year. I usually underwrite a much lower increase, but when investing passively, that is my cut-off.

I have seen a few deals, that I've almost invested in, where the income growth from year to year in their underwriting was under 10%. That met my criteria but the sponsor did not provide the T12 on the property. I re-quested and received the financials and could see that the underwritten year one income was a 30% (or more) increase, compared to the T3, so I did not invest in those deals. That is why it's so important to review the financials on a property. The bottom line: no matter what a sponsor has told me, I've never seen anyone achieve this type of growth on a stabilized property.

That 10% is just my guideline; sometimes things change based on market conditions. During the COVID-19 crisis, any deal I acquired or invested in had underwritten zero rental growth over the T3 for at least the first year of ownership.

Fudgeable Factor #3: Expenses

In the underwriting, I like to see a detailed breakdown of all expenses—not everything lumped together in the expenses line item. I want to see the T12 expenses and compare that to the pro forma. I want a really good explanation for any expenses that are different on the pro forma than the amounts shown in the T12.

One of the things I keep a close eye on is utility charges. They should be the same as on the T12. If the business plan is to implement a conservation or a bill back program, those items will not happen immediately on day one. These programs take time to implement. Be cautious with electric or water conservation programs, as the estimate of savings provided by vendors can be overly optimistic. All of these adjustments should be gradual over time. In the case of implementing bill back (sometimes referred to as a RUBS program) you need to wait for current leases to expire. So, it takes a minimum of one year to put this in place, sometimes longer. I want to dig in and understand exactly what's going on if they're billing back for those utilities. A bill back shouldn't decrease the utility expense in your underwriting, but it should increase your other income. Make sure it's not accounted for twice—double-dipping by lowering the expense and also increasing other income.

The most important thing to look at regarding expenses is property taxes. With the possible exception of payroll, property taxes are going to be the largest single line item on the list of expenses.

The way a property is taxed differs depending on the county where the property is located, but you are almost always going to see an increase, and you want to make sure that increase is taken into account in the underwriting. Most brokers' pro formas do not accurately adjust for the correct lift in property taxes.

As a sponsor myself, I don't rely on the brokers' projection or even the information from the county website. I work with a local tax consultant. These are professionals who contest taxes with that county for a living. They have deep insight into the way a county actually taxes the property and any changes (or proposed changes) to the existing legislation.

While I was underwriting one deal, I found out from a local tax consultant about new legislation being proposed, and likely to pass, that would increase the property tax substantially. The consultant was 80% sure it would pass and this brought in a tremendous amount of additional risk with this new, higher property tax. The deal didn't work on paper anymore, and we ended up walking away from it due to this risk factor.

Often, property tax is based on sales price. Some jurisdictions require a disclosure of real estate transfer prices and some do not. I offer you a word of caution on this. I know that some people are purchasing properties in disclosure areas and buying the properties using a "drop-down entity" so that they're purchasing the entity that owns the property and not the property itself. This is done so that the transaction doesn't get recorded with the new purchase price. They are doing this to circumvent a tax increase, however I hear that many municipalities are getting wise to this scheme. They are actually conducting investigations into all the properties in their county and taking a look at what mortgage is recorded on the properties. They don't see a sale recorded, but they see a new mortgage for a large amount and make a determination based on the amount recorded for the mortgage. They make an assumption that it's a 75% loan and they determine a new value for the property based on this. You may be able to fight this, but you could get into a lengthy court battle.

I want to make sure when I'm investing in a deal that a sponsor is really taking into account what that bump in property taxes will look like. A number of factors can change, so be sure that the team is making an educated assumption based on real data and by speaking with professionals in that field.

The last expense to look at is insurance. Due to the increase in adverse weather phenomena, insurance has been increasing at a very high rate. Make sure your sponsor team is not basing insurance costs on the T12 or some other assumption. They need to have an actual quote for a specific property from a reputable supplier. No exceptions.

Fudgeable Factor #4: Financing

It is crucial to understand the financing for the property. This is a pivotal factor in a deal's success or failure. The myriad types of debt structures range from short term bridge loans to long term agency debt, and there are an unlimited number of specialty products on the market. The type of debt being placed and the terms behind it can have a tremendous effect on your returns.

I often invest in deals where you hold the mortgage debt for longer terms. In the commercial world, this means loans with 10- to 12-year terms. I like this type of loan because I know that the real estate market is unpredictable. As we've discussed before, the only sure thing about real estate is that it's going to go up and it's going to go down. I have no idea when, or for how long, that will happen.

Real estate is cyclical, and while I may be investing in a deal that has a five-year exit plan, it may be that in five years the market is at the bottom of the cycle. We may need to wait out that depressed market, otherwise we could possibly be selling at a loss, or at least not maximizing our gains. That's why I like to see longer-term debt in place so that I know we can hold onto that asset longer if needed. We will have the option to wait for the real estate market to recover and then exit when the real estate market is strong.

When looking at this longer-term debt, "agency debt" is a very popular choice. These are loans that are backed by either Fannie Mae or Freddie Mac and they really are one of the best types of loans available at the time of the writing of this book. They have lots of great features, beyond being longer term. In general, they are usually **non-recourse**, and they are often fixed rate, amortized over 30 years, they usually have an interest-only period, they may be able to include some of your improvement costs, they're assumable, and they have a supplemental loan option available. They also offer lower interest rates for "mission-driven business"—this is better pricing for properties that target workforce residents, or renters who earn a certain percentage (usually 80%) of the area median income.

Backstage Glossary

Non-Recourse: A loan in which the lender cannot come after the borrower personally if the mortgage goes unpaid. Most of these loans are actually "limited recourse" because they contain special clauses that make the borrower personally liable if there is any fraudulent activity.

If you're doing a deal that has a value-add component, having a couple years of interest-only at the beginning of the loan can be very helpful. It increases your cash-on-cash return in those early years while you're executing your business plan. Just make sure you realize you won't be paying down your mortgage balance during this period, and your debt service payments will increase once this period is over. Hopefully, your income will have increased since you executed your plan.

You want to make sure your loan terms are a good fit with your business plan. Remember, we discussed prepayment penalties in Chapter 9 and saw a real-life example of how it affected our returns at sale.

If there's a refinance in the business plan, this is a very big red flag for me. I would definitely have questions and want to delve into it in more detail and really understand what's going on. A refinance can be fantastic if you're doing a buy-and-hold strategy, and you're looking to hold onto something in perpetuity. In a situation like this, you can refinance the property every five to ten years and do phenomenally well. One of the great things with a refinance, as we discussed in Chapter 11 is that it's not a taxable event. The issue I have is with deals that are dependent on that refinance in year three or later to make the cash-on-cash and total returns look attractive. I want a deal that is going to hit my return criteria without a refinance, because the bottom line is that no one knows if a refinance will be possible. Refinancing, or getting a supplemental loan at some point in the future, is a crapshoot. We don't know where rates and the valuation of the property will be in three years, so we really don't know what a refinance might look like, we're just guessing. I prefer to invest in deals that work without a refinance. If we can refinance during the deal and get our capital back faster, then all the better.

THE KEYSTONE CONCEPTS

These keystone concepts are the foundational kernels of wisdom upon which I have built my win-win approach to business and life.

These are my guiding principles.

Keystone Concept #1: Don't Trade Your Time for Money

They say time is money, but actually, time is more valuable than money. You can always find ways to generate more money. You can't generate more time. Instead of working for money, have your money work for you. Once you have enough passive income, you don't have to trade your time for money.

Keystone Concept #2: Be Persistent

Julie Andrews is attributed with saying "Perseverance is failing 19 times and succeeding the 20th." Or as Captain Taggart says in *Galaxy Quest* "Never Give Up, Never Surrender!"

Keystone Concept #3: Learn to Pivot

From Florida to New York. From actor to boutique agency owner. No matter what curveballs life throws your way, stay light on your feet, and be able to change your steps when the dance calls for it.

Keystone Concept #4: Add Value

Figure out how you can add value to both your asset and the community at large. Improving the property and the surrounding community helps increase the value of your asset. This can have a dramatic and positive impact to your bottom line and makes you, as an investor, an asset to your corner of the world.

Keystone Concept #5: Cash Flow Is King

Only buy properties that generate positive cash flow. This gives you the resilience you will need to ride out the inevitable dips in market cycles. Always remember, you never lose money if you never have to sell.

Keystone Concept #6: Teamwork Makes the Dream Work

Build a community of trust and hang on to it like gold. These trusted and knowledgeable advisors are the edge you will need to help influence big decisions, push through times of uncertainty, and lend you their expertise when you need it.

Keystone Concept #7: Follow the Path of Progress

Look for positive signs of social and economic growth. New employers, restaurants, transportation, and housing development are all good indicators that an area is on an upswing and has a good chance to be a wise investment in the future.

Keystone Concept #8: Explore Other Markets

It's okay to invest out of state. Invest where the numbers make sense, even if it's not in your backyard.

Keystone Concept #9: You Want to Be Financially Free

Being debt free is vastly different from being financially free. Don't be afraid to maintain debt in order to increase your investment potential. Use leverage to increase your returns, just do it responsibly.

Keystone Concept #10: Don't Be Afraid of Gurus

Having a mentor or coach, someone who's been there before, can collapse time frames and save you a lot of costly mistakes. Just keep your eyes open and remember to trust but verify.

Keystone Concept #11: A Deal Is Only as Strong as Your Team

Ensure that your project has a strong team with people who have experience operating large scale businesses. There is a big difference between drafting a business plan and actually executing it, and you need people on board who know what they are doing, especially at the beginning.

Keystone Concept #12: The Three Deal Pillars

The three pillars that you need to evaluate when sizing up any deal are: the Sponsor, the Market, and the Deal. The most important one is the sponsor.

Keystone Concept #13: Write Down Your Goals

Set goals and then write them down. Writing them down helps you to understand your mission in a deeper way. The list will serve as a good way to check in with yourself, keep focused, and measure your progress.

Keystone Concept #14: Your Network = Your Net Worth

Start close with family, then friends, then friends of friends. Your network needs to grow organically with you, so be sure to tend to it like a real estate bonsai tree.

Keystone Concept #15: Choose Partners Who Know More Than You Do

Partner up with people who are more experienced than you. You may be able to bring something to the table that compliments their skills and they will bring enormous value because of their greater experience and knowledge. As you grow, reach up and down to help newer investors.

Keystone Concept #16: Luke, Trust Your Feelings

If your gut is telling you something is wrong, listen to yourself. Pull back on the reins until you feel comfortable. You don't have to do anything. Channel your inner Obi-Wan Kenobi and make sure you feel good about everything going on with a deal and don't be afraid to push back or even walk away from the table. If something feels amiss, there is probably a reason.

Keystone Concept #17: Fight for Your Rights

Don't be afraid to stand up for what you believe to be correct, or what you honestly believe your property is worth. Do your math, stand behind your calculations, and be willing to fight for your rights. Sometimes they are worth a small fortune.

Keystone Concept #18: Refinance Responsibly Whenever You Can

Not all debt is bad. In fact, some debt can be downright profitable. Refinancing is a great way to reclaim stored equity in a property and deploy that capital into new investments that can produce more passive income. It can help you achieve your goals faster and, best of all, since you are borrowing the money, it's not considered income and you won't pay taxes on it.

THE BACKSTAGE GLOSSARY
FOR REAL ESTATE

1031 Exchange (pages 124): This allows you to defer (not eliminate) paying taxes on the profits from a sale of property provided you purchase a similar property of equal or greater value. There are strict guidelines and timing requirements that must be adhered to in order to utilize this tax deferment strategy. The name comes from Section 1031 of the U.S. Tax Code where the rules for it are defined, but it's also known as a "Like Kind Exchange" or "Tax Deferred Exchange."

506(b) (page 220): A subsection of SEC Regulation D that allows for accredited and up to 35 sophisticated investors to participate in exempt offerings provided the investor has a preexisting and substantive relationship with the sponsor.

506(c) (page 222): A subsection of SEC Regulation D that allows for only accredited investors to participate in exempt offerings.

Accredited Investor (page 128): A person with an individual or joint net worth (with a spouse) of more than $1 million, excluding their primary residence. Or, someone who in each of the last two years has had an individual income in excess of $200,000—or a joint income (with a spouse) in excess of $300,000—and reasonably expects to continue to reach that income level. As of August 2020, the SEC also defined measures of professional knowledge, experience, or certifications in addition to the tests for income or net worth.

Air Rights (page 83): Development rights that can be transferred to a neighboring property. These grant the owner the right to build additional square footage on their property. When someone sells air rights, they still keep their own property.

Amortization (page 98): The amount of time over which a loan's payments are calculated. This is generally 30 years for a standard single-family home and often shorter for a commercial loan. Commercial loan terms are usually shorter than their amortization, resulting in a large balance that is due at the end of the loan.

Asset (page 40): A thing of value. Think of it as ownership of something that makes you money. Something that generates money that flows to you.

Bonus Depreciation (page 189): Allows you to deduct a large percentage of the purchase price of a property in the first year of ownership.

C.O. (page 67): The Certificate of Occupancy, which is provided by the local authorities to say that a dwelling is built to code and suitable for occupancy. A building inspector will inspect the house (they usually check in at various stages of the construction) and then issue the certificate when work is complete. Without a C.O., no one is legally allowed to stay in the house.

Cap Rate (page 123): The abbreviation of Capitalization Rate. A metric used to evaluate different pieces of real estate under the same terms so as to be able to make an "apples to apples" comparison. The mathematical formula is simply NOI / Property Value. Cap rates remove the financing component and assume that a property is purchased on an all-cash basis. This way, investors understand a property's performance regardless of financing. A property with 95% leverage might have lower cash flow vs. one that has low leverage but the cash flow isn't telling the whole story. Cap rate levels the playing field so deals can be compared from an equal starting point.

Capital Call (page 224): When a syndication asks the member to contribute capital into the company. Depending on the operating agreement, these can be mandatory or discretionary.

Cash Flow (page 11): The movement of money. Positive cash flow is profit that you have after you've received income from an asset and paid for all of its expenses.

Cash-on-Cash Return (page 97): The profit that is made based on the amount of cash that was invested into a deal. If you buy a $60,000 house that costs you $20,000 (down payment and closing costs) and the property gives you $2,000 of positive cash flow each year, that would be a 10% Cash-on-Cash return. ($2,000 / $20,000 = 10%)

Co-op (page 20): A multi-unit building that is owned collectively by the owners. While all the units are owned co-operatively, each unit has its own proprietary lease assigned to a particular owner. Co-ops have bylaws and are controlled by a co-op board consisting of elected members. Co-ops have maintenance fees that are paid by members to cover the property's expenses, including property tax.

Comps (page 55): A price listing of comparable properties in the area, used to determine a reasonable price for the property.

Construction Loan (page 64): Loans that are given in increments. As soon as different portions of the construction are complete, there is an inspection, lien waivers are provided, and then you get a "draw" from the loan to cover that portion of the work.

Cost Segregation Study (page 191): A report identifying the various components that make up a property as a whole, and their respective depreciation class lives. This is conducted by a qualified engineer and in compliance with U.S. tax and accounting rules.

Depreciation (page 71)**:** The reduction in the value of a property over time due to wear and tear on the asset.

Depreciable Basis (page 194)**:** The amount of a fixed asset's cost that can be depreciated over time. This amount is the acquisition cost of the asset, which is the purchase price of an asset plus the cost incurred to put the asset into service.

Equity (page 38)**:** The value of a property minus the claims against it, such as a mortgage.

Fannie Mae (page 99)**:** The Federal National Mortgage Association (FNMA) is a U.S. government-sponsored enterprise. It may be referred to as a type of "agency debt." The organization was formed during the Great Depression by the U.S. Congress to expand the mortgage market. Essentially, the organization helps lenders provide debt at favorable interest rates by reducing the lender's risk by guaranteeing the loan.

FAR (page 178)**:** Floor Area Ratio determines how much square footage a building can have as a ratio of the square footage of the land it sits on. The smaller the building's footprint in relation to the land it sits on, the higher you can build.

Freddie Mac (page 99)**:** The Federal Home Loan Mortgage Corporation (FHLMC) is a U.S. government-sponsored enterprise. It may be referred to as a type of "agency debt." The organization was formed in 1970 to complete with Fannie Mae. Essentially, the organization helps lenders provide debt at favorable interest rates by reducing the lender's risk by guaranteeing the loan.

Guarantor (page 160)**:** A key principal or other person who signs an agreement guaranteeing the payment of the loan.

House Hack (page 81)**:** Purchase a two- to four-unit property and live in one unit while renting the other unit(s) to cover or reduce the mortgage payments. After at least one year, you can move out and rent your old unit as well, covering all your expenses (mortgage included) and resulting in a profit—positive cash flow.

Interest (page 66): Money paid to someone in return for allowing you to borrow money from them. This is paid over and above the amount borrowed to compensate the lender. This is usually determined as a certain percentage of the loan amount. That percentage is called the interest rate.

Interest Rate (page 85): The percentage of a loan that is paid over and above the amount borrowed to compensate the lender. The rate can be at a "fixed" amount that doesn't change for the entire loan, or it can be a "floating" rate that changes depending on certain conditions.

IRR (page 156): The Internal Rate of Return, an important metric for investors when evaluating the performance of an investment. IRR measures the return of an investment over time. The exact same return, over a shorter period of time, will result in a higher IRR because you get your money faster. It's important to understand how an IRR functions, because it measures the profitability of a deal by including how long it will take to realize this return.

Key Principal (page 159): A term used by agency lenders (Fannie Mae and Freddie Mac). Often abbreviated as "KP" this person controls or manages a deal, is critical to its success, and may sign as a guarantor on a loan.

Liability (page 39): Something you owe money for. Think of it as ownership of anything that costs you money. Money that flows away from you.

LOI (page 147): Letter of Intent. A non-legal document that is a written offer on the property. The document details major deal points to make sure the buyer and seller are in agreement. Having an LOI in place ensures both parties are in agreement on the deal points before retaining lawyers to draft a sales agreement.

Leverage (page 44): Using borrowed money to increase the potential return of an investment.

Mean Reversion (page 232): Also known as reversion to the mean, this is a financial theory that states that asset prices and volatility of returns eventually revert to their long-term average levels.

Mortgage (page 35): A legal document where a lender gives money to a borrower in exchange for an interest in something of value, usually a property.

MSA (page 137): The Metropolitan Statistical Area, a geographical area defined by the federal Office of Management and Budget (OMB) that represents the metropolitan area of a city.

Net Worth (page 133): The sum total of everything you own (all your assets) minus everything you owe (all your liabilities).

NOI (page 140): Net Operating Income. This is all of the property's income minus all of the expenses. The income includes not just rent but also items like pet rent, application fees, parking fees, any kind of income that's coming into the property. The expenses include items such as payroll, property, insurance, utilities, maintenance, and repairs. NOI does not take into account any debt (mortgage) payments or items like depreciation and partnership expenses.

Non-Recourse (page 240): A loan in which the lender cannot come after the borrower personally if the mortgage goes unpaid. Most of these loans are actually "limited recourse" because they contain special clauses that make the borrower personally liable if there is any fraudulent activity.

Passive Income (page 15): Money that comes to you with no effort on your part. It may take a small amount of effort to set up, but virtually none to maintain. You can literally make money while you sleep. Examples are rental income or the income from business activities in which you do not materially participate.

Partial Asset Disposition (page 193): The removal of the remaining cost of a portion of an asset that is taken out of service. The remaining cost of the disposed assets produces a tax loss because that portion of the cost had not been deducted yet through depreciation.

Positive Carry (page 103): Making a profit on the difference between interest paid and investment earnings. For example, a difference between the interest you are paying on a loan (5%) vs the profit you receive investing those dollars elsewhere (8%) would result in a positive carry (3%).

Property Classes (A, B, C & D) (page 115): A non-standard classification of properties based on the age of their construction and current condition. While there is no specific set of rules, they are generally grouped as: Class A being constructed within the last 10 years, in great condition, and a top-notch set of amenities. Class B properties are 10 to 30 years old, in good condition, and in good locations. Class C Properties are 30 years or older with a greater need for repairs and maintenance and are generally located in less affluent areas. Class D properties are also 30 year or older but have a significant amount of deferred maintenance and are often located in high crime areas.

PFS (page 133): Your Personal Financial Statement details all of your assets and liabilities. This is required by most lenders in order to get a mortgage; it can provide a clear and concise picture of all your finances.

QI (page 185): A Qualified Intermediary is someone who acts as an intermediary following certain sections of the U.S. Internal Revenue Code. They enter into a withholding agreement with the IRS and are allowed to facilitate certain types of transactions such as a 1031 exchange.

QRP (page 119): A Qualified Retirement Plan, recognized by the IRS, where your money can grow with special tax advantages. Taxes can be deferred, or in the case of a Roth, your money can grow tax free. Most plans offered from an employer, like a 401(k), are qualified plans.

Real Estate Professional (page 192): To reach this classification by the IRS, you must work 750 hours per year in real estate and you must work in this field more than any other work for the year. There are many additional nuances to this classification, so be sure to check with a qualified tax professional to see if it applies to you.

Regulation D (page 220): A Securities and Exchange Commission regulation that allows a project to be considered exempt from having to be registered as a Security with the SEC.

Return on Capital (page 228): Returns that are received by the investor but are not deducted from their capital account.

Return of Capital (page 228): Returns received by the investor that are deducted from their capital account.

ROI (page 44): Return on investment is a measurement of how much profit is made over the entire lifetime of an investment. It does not take into account the length of time your money is invested.

SDIRA (page 118): A self-directed individual retirement account is an account that can hold a variety of alternative investments normally unavailable in an IRA. Although the account is administered by a custodian or trustee, it is directly managed by the account holder—the reason it's called self-directed.

SEC (page 110): The Securities and Exchange Commission (SEC) was created following the 1929 stock market crash. It is a part of the federal government that protects investors.

Security (page 220): A financial instrument that holds monetary value. It can be in the form of equity, debt, or a hybrid, and is regulated by the SEC.

Sophisticated Investor (page 221): Someone with sufficient knowledge and experience in financial and business matters to make them capable of evaluating the merits and risks of the prospective investment. Unlike an Accredited Investor, the SEC does not have financial thresholds to meet this status.

Sponsor (page 111): A person who leads a syndication. May also be called a "syndicator" or "general partner." There is often more than one sponsor on a deal. They can have different roles, ranging from the identification and acquisition of properties, through the operation and ultimate disposition of the property.

Step-Up in Basis (page 183): An adjustment to the value of an asset for tax purposes when it passes from an owner to their heir.

Syndication (page 109): The pooling of capital and resources among multiple investors to achieve a common goal.

T12 (page 230): A financial report showing the trailing 12 months of profit and loss, broken down by month. The trailing 3 months is referred to as the T3.

Tax Lien (page 89): A lien placed on a property to ensure the payment of taxes. The laws vary from state to state, but purchasing these liens from the municipalities that impose them can result in very large returns or possibly ownership of the property.

UBIT (page 119): Unrelated Business Income Tax is a tax that is imposed on a tax-exempt organization that is not related to the tax-exempt purpose of that organization. If you invest in a property that utilizes debt (a mortgage) then you may be subject to tax on the gains attributed to that mortgage. For example, if a property is purchased with a 75% mortgage, then 75% of your gains are subject to tax.